Homework and Practice Workbook

HOLT

MIDDLE SCHOOL Math

Course 3

ADDITIONAL PRACTICE FOR EACH LESSON

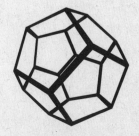

Holt
Middle School Math

Homework and Practice
Course 3

HOLT, RINEHART AND WINSTON

A Harcourt Education Company

Austin • Orlando • Chicago • New York • Toronto • London • San Diego

Printed in the United States of America

ISBN 0-03-065186-7

24 25 0956 12 11 10

CONTENTS

Holt Middle School Math

CONTENTS, *CONTINUED*

Holt Middle School Math

Homework and Practice

LESSON 1-1 *Variables and Expressions*

Evaluate each expression for the given value of the variable.

1. $5x - 3$ for $x = 4$

2. $23 - b$ for $b = 16$

_____

_____

3. $\frac{1}{2}y$ for $y = 22$

4. $19 - 3x$ for $x = 6$

_____

_____

5. $7b - 9$ for $b = 9$

6. $8.6 + 9y$ for $y = 7$

_____

_____

7. $78 - 14k$ for $k = 5$

8. $9(a + 3)$ for $a = 6$

_____

_____

Evaluate each expression for the given value of the variables.

9. $3x + y$ for $x = 6$ and $y = 9$

10. $5a - b$ for $a = 6$ and $b = 8$

_____

_____

11. $7m - 8n$ for $m = 10$ and $n = 7$

12. $7r + 6s$ for $r = 12$ and $s = 14$

_____

_____

13. $10(x - y)$ for $x = 14$ and $y = 8$

14. $m(18 - x)$ for $m = 9$ and $x = 6$

_____

_____

A caterer determines $\frac{1}{4}$ pound of roast beef is needed to serve each guest at a party. How many pounds of roast beef are needed for each number of guests?

15. 8 guests

16. 12 guests

17. 18 guests

18. 25 guests

_____

_____

_____

_____

Holt Middle School Math

LESSON
1-2

Homework and Practice
Writing Algebraic Expressions

Write an expression for each word phrase.

1. a number *x* divided by 7

   _____

2. the sum of 10 and a number *n*

   _____

3. a number *b* decreased by 14

   _____

4. the product of a number *x* and 8

   _____

5. 12 times the difference of a number *r* and 7

   _____

6. 11 minus the product of 5 and a number *k*

   _____

7. **a.** Grace wants to divide the job of writing *x* invitations to the party equally among 4 committee members. Write an expression to determine the number of invitations she will have each committee member write.

   _____

   b. If Grace has 220 invitations for the committee members to write, how many will she have each member write?

   _____

Write an algebraic expression and use it to evaluate each word problem.

8. Arturo purchased a package of 50 blank CDs. After he used *x* CDs, he had *x* less than 50 CDs remaining. How many CDs did he have left after using 31 CDs?

   _____

9. At the grocery store, Henry bought *c* pounds of cashews for $4.99 per pound. If he buys 2 pounds, how much will they cost?

   _____

Holt Middle School Math

LESSON 1-3 Homework and Practice
Solving Equations by Adding or Subtracting

Determine which value is a solution of the equation.

1. $x - 8 = 14$; $x = 6, 20,$ or 22

_____

2. $8 + a = 19$; $a = 7, 11,$ or 27

_____

3. $y - 14 = 22$; $y = 8, 12,$ or 36

_____

4. $d + 17 = 52$; $d = 25, 35,$ or 69

_____

Solve.

5. $m - 9 = 14$

_____

6. $7 + x = 16$

_____

7. $k + 12 = 31$

_____

8. $y - 14 = 46$

_____

9. $13 + r = 29$

_____

10. $17 + t = 19$

_____

11. $b + 39 = 57$

_____

12. $p + 27 = 27$

_____

13. $0 = w - 45$

_____

14. $8.7 + s = 12.1$

_____

15. $x - 3.7 = 0.8$

_____

16. $n - 3.41 = 5.40$

_____

17. The school library is combining books from two storage units into a newly designed area for the library. The first original unit held 186 books and the second unit had 307 books. Write and solve an equation to find the number of books in the new area of the library.

_____

18. Amelia wanted to buy a new computer and printer which had a total cost of $1099.95. She had saved $389.85 for her purchase. How much more does she need to save to buy the computer and printer she wants?

_____

Holt Middle School Math

Name _____ Date _____ Class _____

Homework and Practice
Solving Equations by Multiplying and Dividing

Solve.

1. $7n = 49$

2. $6w = 48$

3. $3a = 39$

_____

_____

_____

4. $\dfrac{b}{5} = 10$

5. $\dfrac{x}{7} = 13$

6. $\dfrac{c}{24} = 6$

_____

_____

_____

7. $12n = 96$

8. $57 = 3k$

9. $22x = 176$

_____

_____

_____

10. $\dfrac{w}{22} = 17$

11. $\dfrac{h}{16} = 16$

12. $13 = \dfrac{t}{33}$

_____

_____

_____

13. $572 = 26m$

14. $\dfrac{x}{24} = 18$

15. $46v = 828$

_____

_____

_____

16. $2x + 3 = 19$

17. $\dfrac{r}{2} + 7 = 14$

18. $3 = 4s - 5$

_____

_____

_____

19. Ashley saves $32 from her weekly paycheck for her college education. This is $\dfrac{1}{5}$ of her weekly salary. How much does she earn each week? Write and solve an equation to determine the amount Ashley earns each week.

_____

20. Hunter bought a package of 24 pencils for $3.12. Write and solve an equation to determine the cost of each pencil in the package.

_____

LESSON 1-5 Homework and Practice
Solving Simple Inequalities

Use <, >, or = to compare each inequality.

1. $8 + 13 \;\square\; 20$

2. $23 \;\square\; 3(7)$

3. $28 - 9 \;\square\; 18$

4. $67 \;\square\; 9(8)$

5. $52 - 37 \;\square\; 15$

6. $78 \;\square\; 12(6)$

Solve and graph each inequality.

7. $x + 3 > 7$

_____

8. $y - 5 \leq 1$

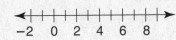

_____

9. $4n \geq 20$

_____

10. $h - 1 \geq 6$

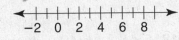

_____

11. $\dfrac{x}{5} < 3$

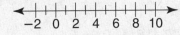

_____

12. $\dfrac{t}{3} \geq 4$

_____

13. $9d > 45$

_____

14. $17 + m < 23$

_____

15. $128 \geq 16x$

_____

16. Philippe wants to drink at least 72 ounces of water every day while at work. He works 6 hours a day. How many ounces of water must Philippe drink each hour? Write and solve an inequality to answer the question.

_____

17. Glynn's car has a 18 gallon gas tank. He travels 450 miles. What is the least miles per gallon Glynn's car will get on this trip? Write and solve an inequality to answer the question.

_____

Holt Middle School Math

Name _____ Date _____ Class _____

Homework and Practice
Combining Like Terms

Combine like terms.

1. $11b + 6b$

2. $9m - 3m$

3. $5x + 8x + 7$

_____

_____

_____

4. $8w + 9x + 7w$

5. $13r + 10r - 8t$

6. $9g + 4m - 8g$

_____

_____

_____

7. $12b + 14p - 7$

8. $7a + 11a - a$

9. $15 + 3x - 9 + 8x$

_____

_____

_____

10. $6x + y + x + 9y$

11. $8m + 14 + 7m - 11$

12. $13x - 4 - 12x + 9$

_____

_____

_____

Simplify.

13. $5(x + 4) - 7$

14. $9(6 + y) + 3y$

15. $6(7 + 2a) - 8a$

_____

_____

_____

Solve.

16. $5r + 2r = 21$

17. $15t - 9t = 54$

18. $6x + 8x = 42$

_____

_____

_____

19. Janelle has d dimes and n nickels. Her sister has 5 times as many dimes and 6 times as many nickels as Janelle has. Write the sum of the number of coins they have, and then combine like terms.

_____

20. If Janelle has 9 dimes and 18 nickels, how many total coins do Janelle and her sister have?

_____

Holt Middle School Math

Homework and Practice

LESSON 1-7 *Ordered Pairs*

Determine whether each ordered pair is a solution of $y = 5 + 3x$.

1. (1, 8)   **2.** (3, 7)   **3.** (2, 10)   **4.** (0, 5)

_____   _____   _____   _____

Determine whether each ordered pair is a solution of $y = 4x - 1$.

5. (0, 1)   **6.** (1, 3)   **7.** (3, 11)   **8.** (5, 19)

_____   _____   _____   _____

Use the given values to complete the table of solutions.

9. $y = x + 4$ for $x = 0, 1, 2, 3, 4$

x	x + 4	y	(x, y)
0			
1			
2			
3			
4			

10. $y = 2x + 3$ for $x = 0, 1, 3, 5, 7$

x	2x + 3	y	(x, y)
0			
1			
3			
5			
7			

11. $y = 4x - 1$ for $x = 1, 2, 4, 5, 8$

x	4x - 1	y	(x, y)
1			
2			
4			
5			
8			

12. $y = 5x + 2$ for $x = 0, 2, 4, 6, 8$

x	5x + 2	y	(x, y)
0			
2			
4			
6			
8			

13. Mrs. Frank had 150 customers when she began her delivery route. Each month she adds 5 new customers. The equation that gives the total number of customers, *t,* in her route is $t = 150 + 5m$, where *m* is the number of months since she began the route. How many customers will Mrs. Frank have after 12 months?

_____

Holt Middle School Math

Name _____ Date _____ Class _____

Homework and Practice
Graphing on a Coordinate Plane

Give the coordinates of each point.

1. A

2. D

_____   _____

3. H

4. C

_____   _____

5. B

6. T

_____   _____

7. M

8. R

_____   _____

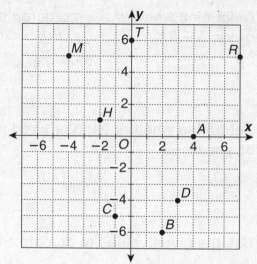

Graph each point on a coordinate plane. Label points A–F.

9. A(3, 5)

10. B(−6, 3)

11. C(0, −4)

12. D(−4, −6)

13. E(5, −2)

14. F(2, 0)

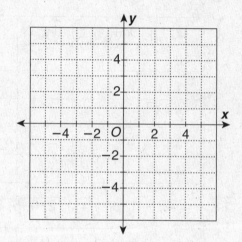

Complete the table of ordered pairs. Graph the equation on a coordinate plane.

15. $y = 2x$

x	x	y	(x, y)
1			
2			
3			

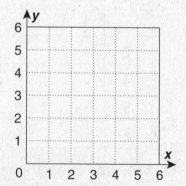

16. A doctor sees 4 patients each hour. Use the equation $y = 4x$, where the y-value represents the many patients that the doctor may see in x hours. Graph, if necessary. How many patients will the doctor see in a 5-hour day?

_____

Holt Middle School Math

Homework and Practice

LESSON
1-9 *Interpreting Graphs and Tables*

The table gives the prices of three different stocks over the first few hours of trading. Tell which stock corresponds to each situation described below.

Time	9:30	10:30	11:30	12:30	1:30
Stock 1	$26.50	$26.00	$25.00	$24.00	$22.50
Stock 2	$38.25	$36.50	$39.75	$37.25	$41.00
Stock 3	$55.00	$55.25	$55.50	$56.00	$57.00

1. A stock opens and rises steadily over the first few hours of trading.

_____

2. A stock opens and declines steadily over the first few hours of trading.

_____

Tell which graph corresponds to each situation in Exercises 1–2.

3.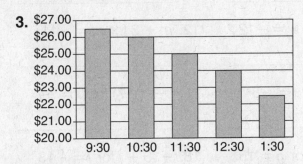

4.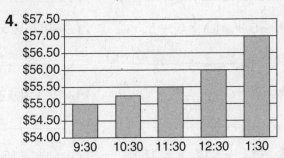

5. Create a graph that illustrates the hours students spent studying for exams.

Student	Number of Hours Studying for Exams
Samantha	3 hours
Seth	3.5 hours
Simon	4 hours
Susan	2.5 hours

Holt Middle School Math

Name _____ Date _____ Class _____

Homework and Practice

Adding Integers

Use a number line to find the sum.

1. $2 + 3$

2. $-5 + 3$

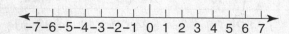

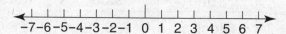

_____

_____

Add.

3. $-6 + 15$

4. $-28 + (-7)$

5. $31 + (-19)$

6. $-34 + 21$

_____   _____   _____   _____

Evaluate each expression for the given value of the variables.

7. $a + 9$ for $a = 5$

8. $x + 7$ for $x = 8$

9. $y + 6$ for $y = 13$

_____   _____   _____

10. $-5 + r$ for $r = -7$

11. $-9 + w$ for $w = -12$

12. $m + 8$ for $m = -11$

_____   _____   _____

13. $-6 + k$ for $k = -9$

14. $t + (-5)$ for $t = -8$

15. $b + (-7)$ for $b = -7$

_____   _____   _____

16. $-11 + x$ for $x = 15$

17. $g + (-15)$ for $g = 15$

18. $-16 + j$ for $j = -18$

_____   _____   _____

19. The music club had 328 members. This year 103 new members joined. How many members does the music club have now?

_____

20. Rosetta is playing a board game with her friends. She rolls doubles of five on her first roll of the number cubes. If a player rolls doubles, they roll again after moving forward. However if they roll doubles again they must move backwards. Rosetta rolls doubles of six on her second roll. How many spaces is Rosetta from her starting place?

_____

Holt Middle School Math

Name _____ Date _____ Class _____

Homework and Practice

Subtracting Integers

Subtract.

1. 9 − 3

2. 12 − 4

3. 9 − 16

4. 19 − 12

_____ _____ _____ _____

5. 7 − 15

6. 18 − 4

7. −8 − 12

8. −11 − 14

_____ _____ _____ _____

9. 25 − 49

10. 18 − 36

11. −101 − 52

12. −76 − (−12)

_____ _____ _____ _____

Evaluate each expression for the given value of the variables.

13. $a − 10$ for $a = 7$

14. $x − 13$ for $x = 20$

15. $17 − y$ for $y = 6$

_____ _____ _____

16. $15 + b$ for $b = −9$

17. $14 − t$ for $t = −18$

18. $d − 24$ for $d = −17$

_____ _____ _____

19. $−16 − w$ for $w = −15$

20. $−10 − r$ for $r = −22$

21. $−14 − g$ for $g = −19$

_____ _____ _____

22. $x − (−18)$ for $x = −25$

23. $y − (−14)$ for $y = −14$

24. $n − (−17)$ for $n = 21$

_____ _____ _____

25. The largest island in the world is Greenland with an area of
839,999 square miles. The second largest island is New Guinea
with an area of 316,615 square miles. What is the difference in
the areas of the two islands?

_____

26. Justin weighed 223 pounds and lost 45 pounds. What is Justin's
new weight?

_____

Holt Middle School Math

LESSON 2-3 Homework and Practice
Multiplying and Dividing Integers

Multiply or divide.

1. 7×9 **2.** $\dfrac{-21}{3}$ **3.** -9×5 **4.** $\dfrac{28}{-7}$

_____   _____   _____   _____

5. $\dfrac{-42}{-6}$ **6.** $-11(-8)$ **7.** $\dfrac{-56}{-8}$ **8.** $4(-13)$

_____   _____   _____   _____

Simplify.

9. $-6(4 + 5)$ **10.** $9(10 - 3)$ **11.** $-7(13 - 4)$ **12.** $8(17 - 11)$

_____   _____   _____   _____

13. $14(-5 + 3)$ **14.** $-10(5 - 14)$ **15.** $11(-15 + 9)$ **16.** $-12(-7 - 3)$

_____   _____   _____   _____

Complete the table for the equation $y = 2x - 3$.
Then plot the points on the coordinate plane.

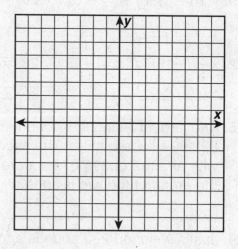

	x	$2x - 3$	y	(x, y)
17.	2			
18.	1			
19.	0			
20.	−1			
21.	−2			

22. Mr. Sweeney's stock portfolio lost $125 for 3 consecutive days. What was the total dollar amount the stock lost over the 3 days?

_____

23. The temperature was –2, –3, 1, and –4 on four consecutive days. What was the average temperature for those days?

_____

Holt Middle School Math

Name _____ Date _____ Class _____

Homework and Practice
Solving Equations Containing Integers

Solve.

1. $x + 8 = 3$

_____

2. $y - 4 = 9$

_____

3. $7w = 35$

_____

4. $\dfrac{n}{-2} = 8$

_____

5. $-8 + t = -6$

_____

6. $\dfrac{a}{-6} = 7$

_____

7. $-9 + k = -15$

_____

8. $-9d = 36$

_____

9. $c - 8 = -17$

_____

10. $\dfrac{m}{7} = 8$

_____

11. $-8 + b = -11$

_____

12. $x - 19 = 19$

_____

13. $-5x = 65$

_____

14. $\dfrac{r}{-6} = -4$

_____

15. $h - 17 = -12$

_____

16. $\dfrac{x}{-6} = -6$

_____

17. $s - 15 = -15$

_____

18. $-64 = -8v$

_____

19. Austin High School had an enrollment of 1,428 students. In May, they graduated 418 students. How many students are still enrolled in the school?

_____

20. Mr. Otten saved $32 each week for 26 weeks. How much did he save in that time?

_____

Holt Middle School Math

Name _____ Date _____ Class _____

Homework and Practice
Solving Inequalities Containing Integers

Solve.

1. $x + 5 < 13$ 2. $6y < -36$ 3. $\dfrac{w}{-4} \geq -8$ 4. $t - 9 > -12$

_____   _____   _____   _____

5. $x + (-8) > 16$ 6. $\dfrac{a}{8} \geq -7$ 7. $b - (-13) < -5$ 8. $-7r \geq -49$

_____   _____   _____   _____

Solve and graph.

9. $17 + x > 13$ 10. $\dfrac{w}{-3} \geq -4$

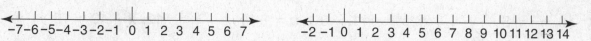

_____   _____

11. $t + (-12) \leq -7$ 12. $-11y < 33$

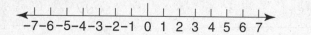   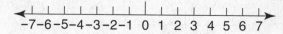

_____   _____

Write an inequality for each of the following.

13. A number increased by negative fifteen is less than twenty-eight.

_____

14. A number multiplied by sixteen is less than or equal to negative thirty.

_____

15. A number divided by twelve is greater than or equal to negative thirty-four.

_____

16. A number decreased by forty-two is greater than thirty-seven.

_____

Holt Middle School Math

Name _____ Date _____ Class _____

Homework and Practice
Exponents

Write using exponents.

1. $8 \times 8 \times 8 \times 8 \times$
$8 \times 8 \times 8$

2. $(-5) \times (-5) \times$
$(-5) \times (-5)$

3. $9 \times 9 \times 9 \times$
$9 \times 9 \times 9$

_____   _____   _____

Evaluate.

4. 10^4

5. $(-4)^3$

6. $(-6)^2$

7. 9^2

_____   _____   _____   _____

8. 14^2

9. $(-8)^2$

10. $(-12)^2$

11. $(-3)^4$

_____   _____   _____   _____

Simplify.

12. $3^3 - 15$

13. $(-4)^4 + 7$

14. $7^2 - 2^5$

15. $78 - 6^2$

_____   _____   _____   _____

16. $11^2 - 3^4 + 3$

17. $16 - 3^3 \times 4$

18. $6^2 + 10 \times 2^4$

19. $-3\,(4^3 + 9^2)$

_____   _____   _____   _____

Evaluate for the given value of the variable.

20. x^3 for $x = -3$

21. $6y^2$ for $y = 4$

22. $w^4 - 17$ for $w = 3$

_____   _____   _____

23. Write an expression for eight times a number used as a factor
four times.

_____

24. If the length of a side of a regular cube is 12 cm, find its volume.
(Hint: $V = l^3$).

_____

15

Holt Middle School Math

Name _____ Date _____ Class _____

Homework and Practice
Properties of Exponents

Multiply. Write the product as one power.

1. $10^6 \times 10^9$ **2.** $a^8 \times a^6$ **3.** $15^6 \times 15^{12}$ **4.** $11^{12} \times 11^7$

_____ _____ _____ _____

5. $(-w)^8 \times (-w)^{12}$ **6.** $(-12)^{18} \times (-12)^{13}$ **7.** $13^{10} \times 13^{15}$ **8.** $w^{14} \times w^{12}$

_____ _____ _____ _____

Divide. Write the quotient as one power.

9. $\dfrac{a^{25}}{a^{18}}$ **10.** $\dfrac{(-13)^{14}}{(-13)^9}$ **11.** $\dfrac{14^{12}}{14^8}$ **12.** $\dfrac{18^{11}}{18^5}$

_____ _____ _____ _____

13. $\dfrac{19^{15}}{19^4}$ **14.** $\dfrac{21^{22}}{21^{20}}$ **15.** $\dfrac{(-x)^{17}}{(-x)^7}$ **16.** $\dfrac{25^8}{25^3}$

_____ _____ _____ _____

Write the product or quotient as one power.

17. $r^9 \times r^8$ **18.** $\dfrac{16^{20}}{16^{10}}$ **19.** $\dfrac{x^{15}}{x^9}$

_____ _____ _____

20. $(-17)^8 \times (-17)^7$ **21.** $27^7 \times 27^6$ **22.** $\dfrac{m^{16}}{m^{10}}$

_____ _____ _____

23. $(-b)^{21} \times (-b)^{14}$ **24.** $\dfrac{26^{17}}{26^5}$ **25.** $(-s)^{11} \times (-s)^4$

_____ _____ _____

26. Hampton has a baseball card collection of 5^6 cards. He organizes the cards into boxes that hold 5^4 each. How many boxes will Hampton need to hold the cards? Write the answer as one power.

_____

27. Write the expression for a number used as a factor seventeen times being multiplied by a number used as a factor fourteen times. Then write the product as one power.

_____

Holt Middle School Math

Homework and Practice
LESSON 2-8 *Looking for a Pattern in Integer Exponents*

Evaluate the powers of 10.

1. 10^{-6}

2. 10^4

3. 10^{-3}

4. 10^5

_____ _____ _____ _____

5. 10^{-1}

6. 10^8

7. 10^{-5}

8. 10^2

_____ _____ _____ _____

Evaluate.

9. $(-7)^{-3}$

10. $\dfrac{11^2}{11^5}$

11. $\dfrac{a^8}{a^{14}}$

_____ _____ _____

12. $(-8)^{-4}$

13. $6^{-3} \cdot 6^{-2}$

14. $\dfrac{5^9}{5^{13}}$

_____ _____ _____

15. $14^{-2} \cdot 14^5$

16. $\dfrac{19^7}{19^9}$

17. $\dfrac{(-15)}{(-15)^4}$

_____ _____ _____

18. $(-17)^{-3} \cdot (-17)^6$

19. $\dfrac{21^2}{21^4}$

20. $(20)^3 \cdot (20)^{-5}$

_____ _____ _____

Express the answer using powers of 10 and negative numbers.

21. 1 meter = $\dfrac{1}{1000}$ km = _____ km.

22. Find the volume of a cube with a side that measures 0.01 cm.
(Hint: $V = s^3$).

_____

Holt Middle School Math

Homework and Practice
LESSON
2-9 *Scientific Notation*

Write each number in standard notation.

1. 6.12×10^2 **2.** 7.9×10^{-3} **3.** 4.87×10^4 **4.** 9.3×10^{-2}

_____   _____   _____   _____

5. 8.06×10^3 **6.** 5.7×10^{-4} **7.** 3.17×10^{-5} **8.** 9.00613×10^{-2}

_____   _____   _____   _____

9. 9.85×10^{-5} **10.** 6.004×10^7 **11.** 8.23×10^4 **12.** 1.48×10^{-6}

_____   _____   _____   _____

Write each number in scientific notation.

13. 108,000,000   **14.** 0.5943   **15.** 42   **16.** 0.0000673

_____   _____   _____   _____

17. 0.0056   **18.** 6004   **19.** 0.00852   **20.** 24,631,500

_____   _____   _____   _____

21. 89450   **22.** 0.005702   **23.** 8,005,000,000   **24.** 0.00012805

_____   _____   _____   _____

25. The mass of the Earth is 5,980,000,000,000,000,000,000,000 kilograms. Write this number in scientific notation.

_____

26. The mass of a dust particle is 7.53×10^{-10}. Write this number in standard notation.

_____

Holt Middle School Math

Homework and Practice

LESSON
3-1

Rational Numbers

Simplify.

1. $\frac{6}{12}$

2. $\frac{6}{24}$

3. $\frac{12}{36}$

4. $-\frac{8}{32}$

_____ _____ _____ _____

5. $\frac{15}{27}$

6. $-\frac{16}{24}$

7. $-\frac{12}{96}$

8. $\frac{12}{54}$

_____ _____ _____ _____

Write each decimal as a fraction in simplest form.

9. 0.56

10. 3.2

11. 0.036

12. −2.05

_____ _____ _____ _____

13. 3.502

14. 0.064

15. −8.4

16. 0.004

_____ _____ _____ _____

17. −0.70

18. 5.25

19. 0.128

20. 0.0004

_____ _____ _____ _____

Write each fraction as a decimal.

21. $\frac{3}{8}$

22. $\frac{5}{9}$

23. $\frac{21}{8}$

24. $\frac{17}{18}$

_____ _____ _____ _____

25. $\frac{19}{3}$

26. $\frac{11}{20}$

27. $\frac{7}{5}$

28. $\frac{54}{36}$

_____ _____ _____ _____

29. Make up a fraction that cannot be simplified that has 25 as its denominator.

_____

Holt Middle School Math

Name _____ Date _____ Class _____

LESSON 3-2 Homework and Practice
Adding and Subtracting Rational Numbers

1. Benjamin paid his cell phone bill that was $25.95. He wrote a check that cost $0.75 to pay the bill. When he mailed it, Benjamin put a $0.37 stamp on the letter. What was the total cost for Benjamin to pay his cell phone bill?

_____

2. Dannika is preparing a recipe that calls for $2\frac{3}{4}$ cups of flour. If Dannika has only $2\frac{1}{4}$ cups left in the flour container, how much flour must she add from a new bag to complete the recipe?

_____

Use a number line to find each sum.

3. $-0.3 + 0.8$

4. $-\frac{4}{5} + \frac{3}{5}$

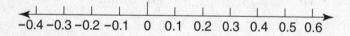

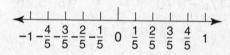

_____   _____

Add or subtract. Write answers in simplest form.

5. $\frac{5}{7} + \frac{1}{7}$

6. $-\frac{1}{8} - \frac{5}{8}$

7. $\frac{5}{12} - \frac{1}{12}$

8. $\frac{3}{16} + \frac{5}{16}$

_____   _____   _____   _____

9. $\frac{2}{15} - \frac{8}{15}$

10. $\frac{7}{20} - \frac{3}{20}$

11. $-\frac{5}{18} - \frac{7}{18}$

12. $-\frac{3}{25} + \frac{11}{25}$

_____   _____   _____   _____

Evaluate each expression for the given value of the variable.

13. $92.7 + x$ for $x = 4.8$

14. $27.3 + x$ for $x = -9.5$

15. $\frac{5}{24} + x$ for $x = -\frac{7}{24}$

_____   _____   _____

Holt Middle School Math

Homework and Practice

LESSON 3-3
Multiplying Rational Numbers

Multiply. Write each answer in simplest form.

1. $6\left(\dfrac{2}{3}\right)$

2. $-9\left(\dfrac{1}{3}\right)$

3. $-8\left(-\dfrac{3}{16}\right)$

4. $-14\left(\dfrac{3}{7}\right)$

_____ _____ _____ _____

5. $\dfrac{5}{12}\left(-\dfrac{6}{25}\right)$

6. $-\dfrac{1}{12}\left(\dfrac{18}{5}\right)$

7. $\dfrac{1}{3}\left(\dfrac{18}{2}\right)$

8. $-\dfrac{5}{12}\left(-\dfrac{6}{15}\right)$

_____ _____ _____ _____

9. $-\dfrac{5}{6}\left(-\dfrac{12}{20}\right)$

10. $\dfrac{7}{24}\left(-\dfrac{12}{35}\right)$

11. $\dfrac{19}{24}\left(-\dfrac{12}{57}\right)$

12. $\dfrac{18}{33}\left(-\dfrac{11}{54}\right)$

_____ _____ _____ _____

Multiply.

13. $3.1(2.6)$

14. $-0.72(0.05)$

15. $(8)(-5.8)$

16. $-4(-5.56)$

_____ _____ _____ _____

17. $-0.08(-6.02)$

18. $0.7(-9.3)$

19. $(-1.14)(9.5)$

20. $(-6.5)(-3.6)$

_____ _____ _____ _____

21. $18(-0.15)$

22. $(-4.32)(7.1)$

23. $-11.3(-6.2)$

24. $(8.516)(3.25)$

_____ _____ _____ _____

Evaluate $3\dfrac{1}{4}x$ for each value of x.

25. $x = -3$

26. $x = -\dfrac{2}{3}$

27. $x = 2$

28. $x = \dfrac{1}{2}$

_____ _____ _____ _____

29. Blaine repaired a damaged car in $8\dfrac{1}{2}$ hours. He received \$26.50 an hour for his work. How much was Blaine paid for repairing the car?

_____

Holt Middle School Math

Name _____ Date _____ Class _____

Homework and Practice
Dividing Rational Numbers

Divide. Write each answer in simplest form.

1. $\dfrac{1}{4} \div \dfrac{5}{8}$

2. $-\dfrac{5}{6} \div \dfrac{5}{12}$

3. $-\dfrac{2}{5} \div \dfrac{7}{10}$

4. $-\dfrac{3}{14} \div \left(-\dfrac{6}{7}\right)$

_____ _____ _____ _____

5. $\dfrac{7}{9} \div \left(\dfrac{5}{6}\right)$

6. $\dfrac{9}{20} \div \left(-\dfrac{3}{4}\right)$

7. $-\dfrac{11}{12} \div \left(-\dfrac{44}{54}\right)$

8. $-\dfrac{13}{30} \div \left(\dfrac{39}{45}\right)$

_____ _____ _____ _____

9. $20 \div \dfrac{4}{9}$

10. $\dfrac{7}{8} \div (-21)$

11. $-10 \div \dfrac{4}{5}$

12. $-\dfrac{21}{25} \div (-14)$

_____ _____ _____ _____

Divide.

13. $32 \div 0.4$

14. $-6.58 \div 0.08$

15. $7.26 \div (-0.03)$

16. $3.333 \div 0.66$

_____ _____ _____ _____

17. $0.0096 \div (-1.2)$ 18. $-25.28 \div 1.6$ 19. $17.5 \div 0.07$

20. $279.4 \div 12.7$

_____ _____ _____ _____

21. $71.46 \div 9$

22. $36.3 \div (-1.6)$

23. $-984.6 \div 2.4$

24. $-601.96 \div 2.02$

_____ _____ _____ _____

Evaluate each expression for the given value of the variable.

25. $\dfrac{52}{x}$ for $x = -0.16$

26. $\dfrac{-14.52}{x}$ for $x = 5.5$

27. $\dfrac{-54.72}{x}$ for $x = -0.003$

_____ _____ _____

28. A 3.6-pound beef roast cost $10.62. What is the cost of the beef roast per pound?

_____

Holt Middle School Math

LESSON 3-5 Homework and Practice
Adding and Subtracting with Unlike Denominators

Add or subtract. Write the answer in simplest form.

1. $\dfrac{1}{2} - \dfrac{3}{8}$

2. $\dfrac{3}{5} + \dfrac{1}{4}$

3. $\dfrac{7}{9} - \dfrac{5}{12}$

4. $-\dfrac{5}{9} + \dfrac{2}{3}$

_____

5. $\dfrac{3}{10} - \left(-\dfrac{1}{2}\right)$

6. $\dfrac{7}{12} + \left(-\dfrac{5}{15}\right)$

7. $-\dfrac{4}{15} - \dfrac{2}{5}$

8. $\dfrac{5}{12} - \dfrac{2}{5}$

_____

9. $-\dfrac{7}{8} + \dfrac{5}{12}$

10. $-2\dfrac{1}{8} - 3\dfrac{1}{4}$

11. $-4\dfrac{3}{5} + 1\dfrac{2}{3}$

12. $6\dfrac{1}{3} - 4\dfrac{5}{6}$

_____

13. $7 - 5\dfrac{7}{8}$

14. $8\dfrac{1}{6} + \left(-\dfrac{7}{12}\right)$

15. $-16 + \left(-\dfrac{8}{9}\right)$

16. $4\dfrac{7}{10} - 11$

_____

Evaluate each expression for the given value of the variable.

17. $-2\dfrac{5}{8} + x$ for $x = 3\dfrac{1}{4}$

18. $1\dfrac{1}{2} + x$ for $x = -2\dfrac{5}{6}$

19. $-7\dfrac{4}{9} - x$ for $x = -7$

_____

20. $9\dfrac{5}{8} + x$ for $x = 6\dfrac{3}{4}$

21. $-15\dfrac{3}{8} + x$ for $x = 1\dfrac{3}{4}$

22. $-15\dfrac{2}{9} - x$ for $x = -12\dfrac{2}{3}$

_____

23. Brendan practiced soccer for $1\dfrac{1}{2}$ hours on Monday, $1\dfrac{1}{4}$ hours on Tuesday, $1\dfrac{1}{6}$ hours on Wednesday and $\dfrac{3}{4}$ hours on Thursday in preparation for the game on Friday. How many total hours did Brendan practice soccer in this week?

_____

Holt Middle School Math

Name _____ Date _____ Class _____

Homework and Practice
Solving Equations with Rational Numbers

Solve.

1. $y - 3.2 = -4.7$

2. $x + 5.61 = 3.89$

3. $0.4d = 8.2$

_____ _____ _____

4. $b - 2 = 17.5$

5. $a + 101 = -14.2$

6. $3.3x = -108.9$

_____ _____ _____

7. $-19.48 + x = -28.03$

8. $\frac{m}{10.1} = 3.5$

9. $217.25 = 39.5w$

_____ _____ _____

10. $\frac{t}{4.7} = -14.7$

11. $b - 29.15 = -17.73$

12. $\frac{r}{-7.6} = 3.05$

_____ _____ _____

Solve. Write each in simplest form.

13. $\frac{5}{8} + y = 2\frac{3}{8}$

14. $\frac{12}{25} m = -\frac{9}{50}$

15. $\frac{6}{35} r = \frac{18}{25}$

_____ _____ _____

16. $x - \left(-\frac{7}{10}\right) = 3\frac{3}{5}$

17. $y - \frac{11}{18} = 4\frac{2}{9}$

18. $-\frac{9}{24} w = \frac{18}{32}$

_____ _____ _____

19. Jessica baked 10 dozen cookies. She left $\frac{1}{8}$ of the baked cookies home and took the rest to school for the bake sale. How many cookies did Jessica take to school?

_____

20. Doug must take 1.25 milliliters of medicine every day. How many days will the medicine last if Doug was given a prescription of the medicine in a bottle containing 50 milliliters?

_____

Holt Middle School Math

Homework and Practice

LESSON 3-7

Solving Inequalities with Rational Numbers

Solve.

1. $-15.7 + y < 9.4$

2. $\dfrac{x}{-2.5} < -1.54$

3. $-6.2t \le 14.57$

_____ _____ _____

4. $\dfrac{x}{4.56} \ge -18.5$

5. $-16.87 + h \le -15.92$

6. $-8.3w \ge -350.26$

_____ _____ _____

Solve. Write answers in simplest form.

7. $w + \dfrac{9}{14} \ge \dfrac{5}{14}$

8. $x - \dfrac{11}{15} > \dfrac{4}{5}$

9. $-\dfrac{10}{21}n \ge -2\dfrac{4}{7}$

_____ _____ _____

10. $4\dfrac{2}{3} y \le -2\dfrac{4}{9}$

11. $\dfrac{x}{-14} < \dfrac{15}{28}$

12. $a - 1\dfrac{7}{18} < -2\dfrac{5}{6}$

_____ _____ _____

13. $d - \left(-2\dfrac{8}{15}\right) > -3\dfrac{7}{10}$

14. $x + \left(-3\dfrac{7}{12}\right) < -3\dfrac{5}{9}$

15. $-4\dfrac{3}{8} y \le -1\dfrac{3}{7}$

_____ _____ _____

16. Mr. Conner's students made kites in science class. He bought a 500-yd bolt of twine to tie to the kites. If he wants to give each student a piece of twine $33\dfrac{1}{3}$ yards long, what is the maximum number of pieces of twine Mr. Conner will be able to make from the bolt of twine?

_____

Holt Middle School Math

Name _____ Date _____ Class _____

Homework and Practice
Squares and Square Roots

Find the two square roots for each number.

1. 16

2. 9

3. 64

4. 121

_____ _____ _____ _____

5. 36

6. 100

7. 225

8. 400

_____ _____ _____ _____

Evaluate each expression.

9. $\sqrt{27 + 37}$

10. $\sqrt{41 + 59}$

11. $\sqrt{122 - 41}$

12. $\sqrt{167 - 23}$

_____ _____ _____ _____

13. $3\sqrt{81} + 19$

14. $25 - \sqrt{25}$

15. $\sqrt{169} - \sqrt{36}$

16. $\sqrt{196} + 25$

_____ _____ _____ _____

17. $\dfrac{\sqrt{81}}{9}$

18. $-4.9\sqrt{64}$

19. $\dfrac{\sqrt{225}}{\sqrt{25}}$

20. $\dfrac{\sqrt{100}}{-2.5}$

_____ _____ _____ _____

21. Find the product of six and the sum of the square roots of 100 and 225.

_____

22. Find the difference between the square root of 361 and the square root of 289.

_____

23. If a replica of the ancient pyramids were built with a base area of 1,024 in.^{2}, what would be the length of each side? (Hint: $s = \sqrt{A}$)

_____

24. The maximum displacement speed of a boat is found using the formula: Maximum Speed in km/h = 4.5 $\sqrt{\text{the waterline length of the boat in meters}}$. Find the maximum displacement speed of a boat that has a waterline length of 9 meters.

_____

Holt Middle School Math

Homework and Practice

LESSON 3-9 *Finding Square Roots*

Each square root is between two integers. Name the integers.

1. $\sqrt{10}$ **2.** $\sqrt{24}$ **3.** $\sqrt{51}$ **4.** $\sqrt{39}$

_____   _____   _____   _____

5. $\sqrt{66}$ **6.** $\sqrt{30}$ **7.** $\sqrt{78}$ **8.** $\sqrt{87}$

_____   _____   _____   _____

Use a calculator to find each value. Round to the nearest tenth.

9. $\sqrt{18}$ **10.** $\sqrt{63}$ **11.** $\sqrt{19}$ **12.** $\sqrt{41}$

_____   _____   _____   _____

13. $\sqrt{53}$ **14.** $\sqrt{98}$ **15.** $\sqrt{54}$ **16.** $\sqrt{72}$

_____   _____   _____   _____

17. $\sqrt{83}$ **18.** $\sqrt{120}$ **19.** $\sqrt{200}$ **20.** $\sqrt{489}$

21. The distance a person can see at sea is measured in miles by using the formula $d = \sqrt{\dfrac{3}{2}h}$, where h is the height in ft above sea level. About how many miles can a person see that is 8 feet above sea level? Round the answer to the nearest tenth of a mile.

_____

22. The length of the hypotenuse of a right triangle is the square root of the sum of the squares of the measures of the other two legs of the triangle. Approximate the length of the hypotenuse of a right triangle if the legs have measures 12 and 15.

_____

23. At an accident scene, a police officer may determine the rate of speed, r, in mi/h, of the car by using the following formula $r = \sqrt{20\ell}$, where ℓ is length of the skid marks. How fast was a car going if the skid marks at the scene are 180 ft long?

_____

Holt Middle School Math

Homework and Practice
3-10 *The Real Numbers*

Write all names that apply to each number.

1. $\sqrt{\dfrac{36}{4}}$

2. $-\dfrac{3}{16}$

3. $\sqrt{0.81}$

_____   _____   _____

_____   _____   _____

4. -81

5. $-7.23\overline{3}$

6. $\sqrt{95}$

_____   _____   _____

State if the number is rational, irrational, or not a real number.

7. $\sqrt{49}$

8. $-\sqrt{144}$

9. $\dfrac{9}{\sqrt{3}}$

10. $\dfrac{\sqrt{81}}{\sqrt{9}}$

_____   _____   _____   _____

11. $\dfrac{21}{0}$

12. $\dfrac{20}{8}$

13. $\sqrt{-100}$

14. 8.67

_____   _____   _____

Find a real number between each pair of numbers.

15. $4\dfrac{2}{5}$ and $4\dfrac{3}{5}$

16. 7.25 and $\dfrac{15}{2}$

17. $\dfrac{5}{8}$ and $\dfrac{3}{4}$

_____   _____   _____

18. Give an example of a rational number between $-\sqrt{36}$ and $\sqrt{36}$

_____

19. Give an example of an irrational number less than 0.

_____

20. Give an example of a number that is not real.

_____

Holt Middle School Math

Homework and Practice

LESSON 4-1 *Samples and Surveys*

Identify the population and sample. Give a reason why the sample could be biased.

1. The customers at a diner are surveyed to determine the number of times that local people eat out in a week.

   population _____

   sample _____

   possible bias _____

2. At a school with school colors of purple and white, the male students are asked to name their favorite color.

   population _____

   sample _____

   possible bias _____

3. The first one thousand adults at a professional baseball game are surveyed and asked to name their favorite sport.

   population _____

   sample _____

   possible bias _____

Identify the sampling method used.

4. The supervisor of the recreational committee visits 5 of the city's pools and collects water samples from the pools at various times of the day.

   _____

5. Commuters on a subway are selected at random and asked to name their favorite flavor of ice cream.

   _____

6. The register receipt of every 10th shopper at a grocery store is automatically compiled into a data base of the total amount spend and the items purchased.

   _____

Holt Middle School Math

Name _____ Date _____ Class _____

LESSON 4-2 Homework and Practice
Organizing Data

1. Use the given data to make a table.

Two hundred people were asked which was their favorite type of movie—comedy, drama, or action. The men's choices were 10 for comedy, 35 for drama and 55 for action. The women's choices were 45 for comedy, 50 for drama and 5 for action.

List the data values in the stem-and-leaf plot.

2.
```
1 | 2  5  7  8
2 | 0  0  6
3 | 1  1  2  2
4 | 5  6        key: 4 | 5 = 45
```

3.
```
4 | 4  6  8
5 | 0  2  4  6
6 | 7
8 | 1  3  5  7   key: 8 | 1 = 81
```

_____   _____

4. Use the given data to make a stem-and-leaf plot.

Michael's Test Scores					
86	85	92	75	72	94
81	86	94	77	67	80

key:

5. Use the given data to make a back-to-back stem-and-leaf plot.

MLB American League—Central Division 2000–2001 Final Standings		
MLB Team	**Wins**	**Losses**
Cleveland	91	71
Minnesota	85	77
Chicago	83	79
Detroit	66	96
Kansas City	65	97

Wins	Losses

key:

Holt Middle School Math

Homework and Practice
Central Tendency

Find the mean, median, and mode of each data set.

1. 9, 5, 8, 5, 9, 8, 4, 8, 7

mean: _____

median: _____

mode: _____

2. 8.3, 3.8, 4.2, 6.4, 3.9, 7.7, 4.2

mean: _____

median: _____

mode: _____

3. 41, 43, 44, 42, 44, 45, 42, 47, 43, 46

mean: _____

median: _____

mode: _____

4. 2, 27, 6, 47, 22, 6, 11, 8, 52, 6, 25, 19

mean: _____

median: _____

mode: _____

5. The Baylus family's food bills for the last 6 months were $362, $354, $412, $415, $354 and $353. What is the mean, median, and mode of the food bills for this time period?

_____

Use the data to find each answer.

Oceans		
	Area in sq. mi.	**Greatest Known Depth in ft.**
Pacific Ocean	64,000,000	36,198
Atlantic Ocean	31,815,000	30,246
Indian Ocean	25,300,000	24,460
Artic Ocean	5,440,200	18,456

6. Find the mean of the areas in square miles.

_____

7. Find the median of the area in square miles.

_____

8. Find the mean and median of the greatest known depth in feet.

_____

Holt Middle School Math

Name _____ Date _____ Class _____

LESSON 4-4 Homework and Practice
Variability

Find the range and the first and third quartiles for each data set.

1. 52, 36, 41, 48, 55, 31, 57

range: _____

first quartile: _____

third quartile: _____

2. 26, 28, 42, 43, 22, 56, 51, 36

range: _____

first quartile: _____

third quartile: _____

Use the given data to make a box-and-whisker plot.

3. 44, 56, 30, 73, 34, 55, 62, 51

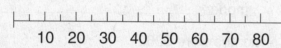

4. 26, 37, 45, 62, 55, 11, 27, 72, 51, 48, 43, 38, 47

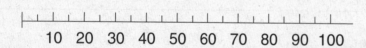

Use the box-and-whisker plots to compare the data sets.

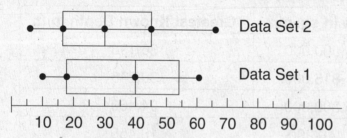

5. Compare the ranges and medians.

_____

_____

6. Compare the ranges of the middle half of the data for each.

_____

_____

Holt Middle School Math

Name _____ Date _____ Class _____

Homework and Practice
Displaying Data

1. Organize the data into a frequency table and make a bar graph.

5 3 8 4 7 8 8 4 8 4 5 7 4 6 5 3 8 7 7 4 8

Number	Frequency

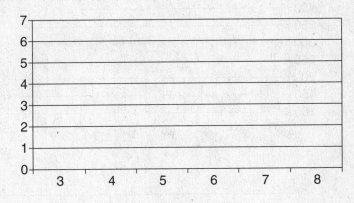

2. Use the data to make a histogram with intervals of 5.

Minutes it takes students to travel to school			
6	10	15	18
10	20	25	20
15	10	8	5
20	15	10	15
18	6	20	15

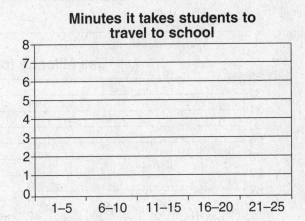

3. Make a line graph of the given data. Use the graph to estimate the percent of food expenses away from home in 1993.

Percent of Food Expenses Away from Home			
1960	19.9%	1980	32.2%
1965	22.8%	1985	35.8%
1970	26.3%	1990	36.7%
1975	28.5%	1995	38.2%

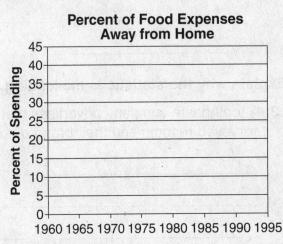

In 1993, approximately _____ % of food expenses were away from the home.

Holt Middle School Math

Name _____ Date _____ Class _____

Homework and Practice
Misleading Graphs and Statistics

Explain why each graph is misleading.

1.

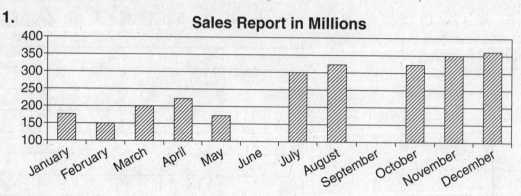

Sales Report in Millions

2.

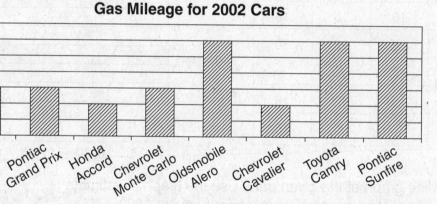

Gas Mileage for 2002 Cars

_____

_____

Explain why the statistic is misleading.

3. A toothpaste company advertises that 9 out of 10 dentists surveyed recommend their brand of toothpaste to their patients.

_____

_____

_____

Holt Middle School Math

Name _____ Date _____ Class _____

Homework and Practice

Scatter Plots

1. Use the given data to make a scatter plot.

Sandwich	Calories	Total Fat Grams
Chicken Breast	318	2
Chicken Teriyaki	374	1.5
Club	323	2
Cold Cut	441	7
Ham	288	1.5
Meatball	527	10
Roast Beef	293	2
Tuna	445	6
Turkey Breast	281	1.5
Veggie	226	1

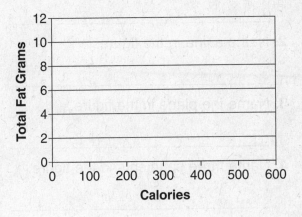

Do the data sets have a positive, a negative, or no correlation?

1. The type of car a person drives and the color of their hair.

_____

3. The number of people working on a job and the hours to completion.

_____

4. The number of innings completed in a baseball game and the number of runs scored.

_____

5. The number of shares of stock owned and the amount received in dividends.

_____

6. Use the data to predict the percent of U.S. Households with a computer in 1998.

Percent of U.S. Households with a Computer			
Year	1985	1990	1995	2000
Percent	8.2%	15%	24.1%	51%

In 1998, about _____% of U.S. households had a computer.

35

Holt Middle School Math

Name _____ Date _____ Class _____

Homework and Practice
Points, Lines, Planes, and Angles

1. Name four points in the figure.

_____

2. Name a line in the figure.

_____

3. Name the plane in the figure.

_____

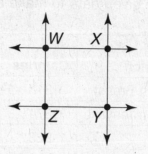

4. Name three segments in the figure.

_____

5. Name four rays in the figure.

_____

6. Name a right angle in the figure.

_____

7. Name two acute angles in the figure

_____

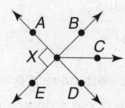

8. Name two obtuse angles in the figure.

_____

9. Name a pair of complementary angles in the figure.

_____

10. Name three pair of supplementary angles in the figure.

_____

In the figure, ∠1 and ∠2 are vertical angles.

11. If $m \angle 1 = 103°$, find $m \angle 2$.

_____

12. If $m \angle 2 = 115°$, find $m \angle 1$.

_____

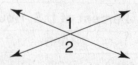

Holt Middle School Math

Homework and Practice
LESSON 5-2 *Parallel and Perpendicular Lines*

1. Measure the angles formed by the transversal and the parallel lines. Which angles seem to be congruent.

_____

_____

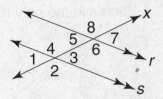

In the figure, line *x* ‖ line *y*. Find the measure of each indicated angle, if the *m* ∠ 8 = 34°.

2. ∠2   **3.** ∠3   **4.** ∠4

_____   _____   _____

5. ∠6   **6.** ∠7   **7.** ∠1

_____   _____   _____

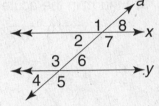

In the figure, line *m* ‖ line *n*. Find the measure of each angle, if *m* ∠ 1 = 131°.

8. ∠2   **9.** ∠3   **10.** ∠4

_____   _____   _____

11. ∠5   **12.** ∠6   **13.** ∠7

_____   _____   _____

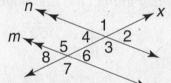

In the figure, line *a* ‖ line *b*.

14. Name all angles congruent to ∠5.

_____

15. Name all angles congruent to ∠4.

_____

16. Name three pairs of angles with sums of 180°.

_____

_____

17. Which line is the transversal?

_____

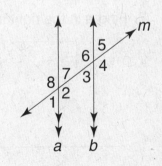

Holt Middle School Math

Name _____ Date _____ Class _____

Homework and Practice
LESSON 5-3 *Triangles*

1. Find *a* in the right triangle.

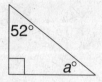

_____

2. Find *b* in the acute triangle.

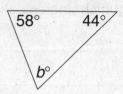

_____

3. Find *m* in the acute triangle.

_____

4. Find *y* in the right triangle.

_____

5. Find *t* in the right triangle.

_____

6. Find *x* in the obtuse triangle

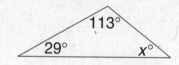

_____

7. Find *a* in the right triangle.

_____

8. Find *x* in the right triangle.

_____

Holt Middle School Math

Name _____ Date _____ Class _____

Homework and Practice
Polygons

Find the sum of the angle measures in each figure.

1.

_____

2.

_____

3.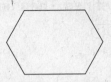

_____

4.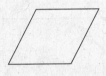

_____

5.

_____

6.

_____

Find the angle measure in each regular polygon.

7.

_____

8.

_____

9.

_____

10.

_____

11.

_____

12.

_____

Write all the names that apply to each figure.

13.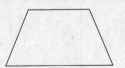

_____

_____

_____

14.

_____

_____

_____

15.

_____

_____

_____

Holt Middle School Math

LESSON 5-5 Homework and Practice
Coordinate Geometry

Determine if the slope of each line is positive, negative, 0, or undefined. Then find the slope of each line.

1. $\overleftrightarrow{AD}$

_____

2. $\overleftrightarrow{BC}$

_____

3. $\overleftrightarrow{MW}$

_____

4. $\overleftrightarrow{TD}$

_____

5. $\overleftrightarrow{SV}$

_____

6. $\overleftrightarrow{RS}$

_____

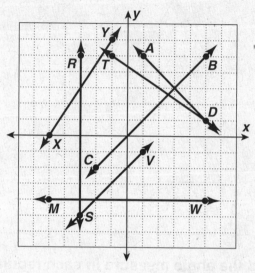

7. Which lines are parallel?

_____

8. Which lines are perpendicular?

_____

Graph the quadrilaterals with the given vertices. Write all the names that apply to each quadrilateral.

9. $(-3, 2)$, $(-6, -4)$, $(4, 2)$, $(6, -4)$

_____

10. $(2, 6)$, $(6, -5)$, $(2, -5)$, $(6, 6)$

_____

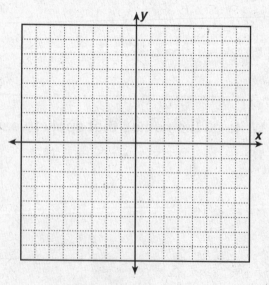

Holt Middle School Math

LESSON 5-6 Homework and Practice
Congruence

Write a congruence statement for each pair of polygons.

1.

_____

2.

_____

3.

_____

4.

_____

Find the value of the variable if triangle *ABC* is congruent to triangle *XYZ*.

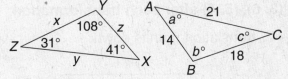

5. Find *a*.   **6.** Find *b*.

_____   _____

7. Find *c*.   **8.** Find *x*.

_____   _____

9. Find *y*.   **10.** Find *z*.

_____   _____

Holt Middle School Math

Name _____ Date _____ Class _____

Homework and Practice
Transformations

Identify each as a translation, rotation, reflection, or none of these.

1.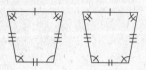

_____

2.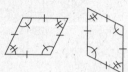

_____

3.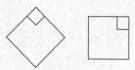

_____

4.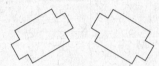

_____

Draw the image of the triangle after each transformation.

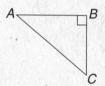

5. reflection across $\overline{BC}$

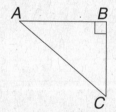

6. translation along $\overline{AB}$ so that C' coincides with B.

Draw the image of the rectangle with vertices $(-1, 6)$, $(-3, 4)$, $(3, 6)$, $(5, 4)$ after each transformation.

7. translation 5 units down

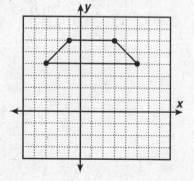

8. 270° clockwise rotation around $(0, 0)$

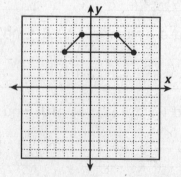

Holt Middle School Math

LESSON 5-8 Homework and Practice
Symmetry

Complete the figure. The dashed line is the line of symmetry.

1.

2.
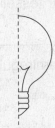

3.

4.

5.
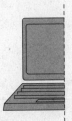

6.

Complete the figure. The point is the center of rotation.

7.

8.

9.

10.

Holt Middle School Math

Name _____ Date _____ Class _____

Homework and Practice
Tessellations

1. Name a possible combination of squares and triangles that would form a semiregular tessellation.

_____

2. Create a semiregular tessellation that uses squares and triangles.

_____

3. Create another semiregular tessellation that uses squares and triangles.

_____

4. Create a tessellation with quadrilateral *ABCD*.

    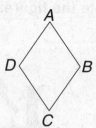

_____

5. Use rotations to create a variation of the tessellation in Exercise 4.

_____

Holt Middle School Math

Name _____ Date _____ Class _____

Homework and Practice
LESSON
6-1 *Perimeter and Area of Rectangles and Parallelograms*

Find the perimeter of each figure.

1.
```
        33
   ┌──────────┐
19 │          │ 19
   └──────────┘
        33
```

2.
```
      24
    ┌──────┐
17 /      / 17
  └──────┘
      24
```

3.
```
      16.25
   ┌────────┐
19.5│       │19.5
   └────────┘
     16.25
```

_____   _____   _____

Graph each figure with the given vertices. Then find the area of each figure.

4. (−4, 3), (−7, −3), (4, −3), (7, 3)   5. (−7, 7), (−7, −7), (7, −7), (7, 7)

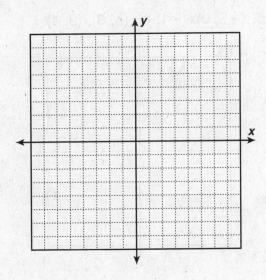   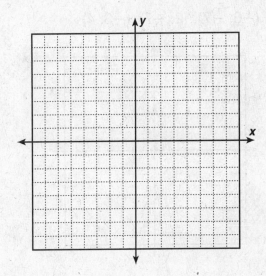

_____   _____

6. Mrs. Delfina is having new carpet installed in a room and hall in her home. The diagram at the right shows the dimensions of the area. If the carpet costs $1.95 a square foot, how much will it cost Mrs. Delfina to carpet the area?

```
         18 ft
    ┌──────────┐
12.5 ft│      │
    │        └────────┐ 3 ft
    └─────────────────┘
           16 ft
```

_____

Holt Middle School Math

Name _____ Date _____ Class _____

Find the perimeter of each figure.

1.
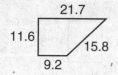

2.
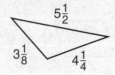

3.
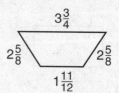

_____ _____ _____

Graph and find the area of each figure with the given vertices.

4. $(-6, -7)$, $(2, -7)$, $(-3, 4)$

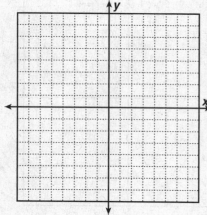

5. $(-5, 0)$, $(-1, 4)$, $(5, 0)$, $(2, 4)$

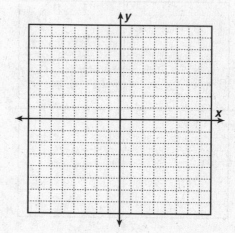

_____ _____

6. $(-1, 7)$, $(4, 7)$, $(-3, -4)$, $(6, -4)$

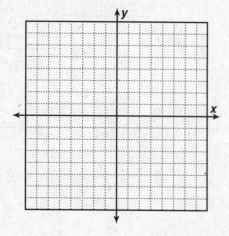

7. $(-6, 2)$, $(6, 2)$, $(6, -4)$

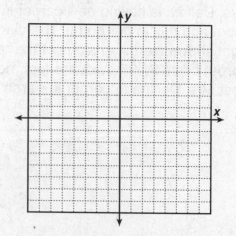

_____ _____

Holt Middle School Math

Name _____ Date _____ Class _____

Homework and Practice

LESSON 6-3

The Pythagorean Theorem

Find the length of the hypotenuse in each triangle.

1.

9

12

_____

2.

24

10

_____

3.

36

27

_____

4. Graph the triangle formed with coordinates (−7, 0), (−7, −6), (1, 0) and find the length of the hypotenuse.

_____

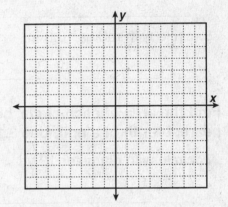

Solve for the unknown side in each right triangle. Round the answers to the nearest hundredth.

5.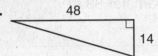

48

14

_____

6.

3.6

2.7

_____

7.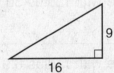

9

16

_____

8.

15

22

_____

9.

28

21

_____

10.

26

24

_____

11.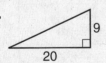

9

20

_____

12.

36

32

_____

13.

34

12

_____

14. Use the Pythagorean Theorem to find the height of the triangle at the right. Then use the height to find the area of the triangle.

65

60

_____

Holt Middle School Math

Name _____ Date _____ Class _____

Find the circumference of each circle, both in terms of π and to the nearest tenth of a unit. Use 3.14 for π.

1. circle with diameter 12 cm

_____

2. circle with radius 11 in.

_____

3. circle with radius 17 ft

_____

4. circle with diameter 28 yd

_____

5. circle with radius 10.8 in.

_____

6. circle with diameter 23.6 m

_____

Find the area of each circle, both in terms of π and to the nearest tenth of a unit. Use 3.14 for π.

7. circle with diameter 12 yd

_____

8. circle with radius 16 cm

_____

9. circle with radius 30 ft

_____

10. circle with diameter 38 m

_____

11. circle with radius 8.9 m

_____

12. circle with diameter 56 m

_____

13. Graph a circle with center (0, 0) that passes through (0, −5). Find the area and circumference, both in terms of π and to the nearest tenth of a unit. Use 3.14 for π.

_____

_____

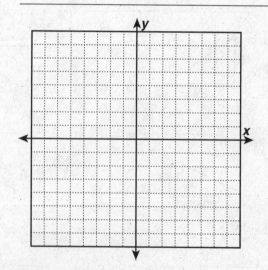

14. If a circle has an area of 7,850 yd², what is the diameter of the circle? Use 3.14 for π.

_____

Holt Middle School Math

Homework and Practice

LESSON 6-5 *Drawing Three-Dimensional Figures*

1. Use isometric dot paper to sketch a rectangular box that is 4 units long, 2 units wide, and 3 units tall.

2. Use isometric dot paper to sketch a cube that is 3 units on each edge.

3. Sketch a one-point perspective drawing of a triangular prism.

4. Sketch a two-point perspective drawing of a rectangular box.

Holt Middle School Math

Name _____ Date _____ Class _____

Homework and Practice

LESSON
6-6

Volume of Prisms and Cylinders

Find the volume to the nearest tenth of a unit. Use 3.14 for π.

1.
8 ft
8 ft
8 ft

_____

2.
10 cm
15 cm

_____

3.
7 yd
8 yd
20 yd

_____

4.
48 mm
36 mm
65 mm

_____

5.
12 in.
23 in.
16 in.

_____

6.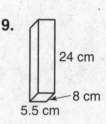
8 cm
21 cm

_____

7.
14.5 in.
14.5 in.
14.5 in.

_____

8.
5 m
12 m
16 m

_____

9.
24 cm
8 cm
5.5 cm

_____

10. A cylinder has a radius of 8 cm and a height of 20 cm. Explain whether tripling the height will triple the volume of the cylinder.

_____

_____

11. Find the height of a cylinder if the volume is 2,512 in.^{3} and the radius is 10 in. Use 3.14 for π.

_____

12. What is the volume of a can of peanuts with a height of 5 in. and a lid that is 4 in. wide? Use 3.14 for π. Round the answer to the nearest tenth of an inch.

_____

_____

Holt Middle School Math

LESSON 6-7 Homework and Practice
Volume of Pyramids and Cones

Find the volume of each figure to the nearest tenth of a unit. Use 3.14 for π.

1.

8 in.

6 in.

_____

2.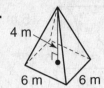

4 m

6 m   6 m

_____

3.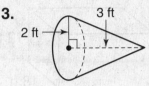

2 ft   3 ft

_____

4.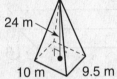

24 m

10 m   9.5 m

_____

5.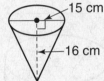

15 cm

16 cm

_____

6.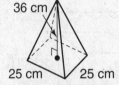

36 cm

25 cm   25 cm

_____

7. A funnel has a diameter of 8 in. and is 21 in. deep. What is the volume of the funnel to the nearest tenth of a unit? Use 3.14 for π

_____

8. The radius of a cone is 13 ft and its height is 27 ft. Find the volume of the cone to the nearest tenth. Use 3.14 for π.

_____

9. Find the volume of a rectangular pyramid if the height is 35 cm and the base sides are 21 cm and 28 cm.

_____

10. The base of a regular pyramid has an area of 135 in.^{2}. The height of the pyramid is 8.5 in. Find the volume.

_____

Holt Middle School Math

Name _____ Date _____ Class _____

Homework and Practice
Surface Area of Prisms and Cylinders

Find the surface area of each figure to the nearest of a tenth unit. Use 3.14 for π.

1.
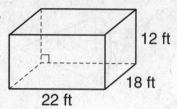
12 ft
18 ft
22 ft

_____

2.
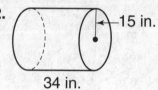
15 in.
34 in.

_____

3.
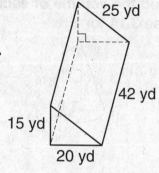
25 yd
42 yd
15 yd
20 yd

_____

4.
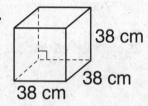
38 cm
38 cm
38 cm

_____

5.
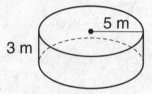
5 m
3 m

_____

6.
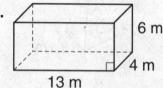
6 m
4 m
13 m

_____

7.
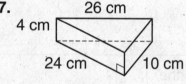
26 cm
4 cm
24 cm
10 cm

_____

8.
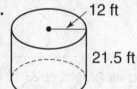
12 ft
21.5 ft

_____

9.
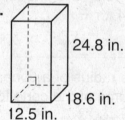
24.8 in.
18.6 in.
12.5 in.

_____

10. Find the surface area to the nearest tenth of a unit of a cylinder
84.5 m tall that has a diameter of 50 m. Use 3.14 for π.

_____

11. Find the surface area to the nearest tenth of a unit of a rectangular
prism with height 24 cm and sides 18 cm and 14 cm.

_____

12. A recipe calls for a 9 × 13 × 2 in. baking dish to have the inside
of the baking dish coated before adding the recipe contents.
What is the surface area of the baking dish that will be coated?

_____

Holt Middle School Math

Homework and Practice

LESSON 6-9

Surface Area of Pyramids and Cones

Find the surface area of each figure to the nearest of a tenth unit. Use 3.14 for π.

1.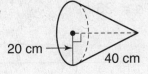
20 cm → 40 cm

_____

2.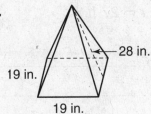
28 in.
19 in.
19 in.

_____

3.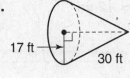
17 ft → 30 ft

_____

4.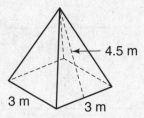
4.5 m
3 m   3 m

_____

5.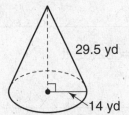
29.5 yd
14 yd

_____

6.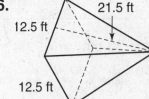
21.5 ft
12.5 ft
12.5 ft

_____

7.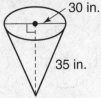
30 in.
35 in.

_____

8.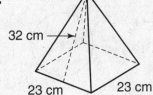
32 cm
23 cm   23 cm

_____

9.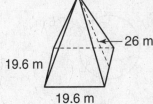
26 m
19.6 m
19.6 m

_____

10. Find the length of the slant height of a square pyramid if the one side of the base is 26 cm and the surface area is 2,236 cm^2.

_____

11. Find the surface area of a regular square pyramid with a slant height of 27 in. and a base perimeter of 96 in.

_____

12. Find the length of the slant height of a cone with a radius of 40 ft and a surface area of 9,420 ft^2. Use 3.14 for π.

_____

Holt Middle School Math

LESSON 6-10 Homework and Practice
Spheres

Find the volume of each sphere, both in terms of π and to the
nearest tenth of a unit. Use 3.14 for π.

1. $r = 12$ yd

_____

_____

2. $r = 27$ ft

_____

_____

3. $d = 36$ m

_____

_____

4. $d = 48$ ft

_____

_____

5. $r = 4.5$ m

_____

_____

6. $r = 7.5$ cm

_____

_____

7. $r = 33$ cm

_____

_____

8. $d = 32.02$ ft

_____

_____

9. $d = 60$ m

_____

_____

Find the surface area of each sphere, in terms of π and to the
nearest tenth of a unit.

10. 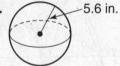 5.6 in.

_____

_____

11. 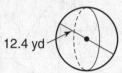 12.4 yd

_____

_____

12. 25 cm

_____

_____

13. 36 ft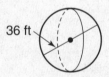

_____

_____

14. 14.1 cm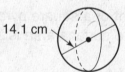

_____

_____

15. 21.5 in.

_____

_____

16. Estimate to the nearest tenth of an inch the surface area of a
baseball with a 3 in. diameter. Use 3.14 for π.

_____

Holt Middle School Math

Name _____ Date _____ Class _____

Homework and Practice

LESSON 7-1
7-1 Ratios and Proportions

Find two ratios that are equivalent to each given ratio.

1. $\dfrac{7}{35}$

2. $\dfrac{4}{16}$

3. $\dfrac{16}{48}$

4. $\dfrac{7}{8}$

5. $\dfrac{24}{6}$

6. $\dfrac{1}{2}$

7. $\dfrac{14}{30}$

8. $\dfrac{16}{6}$

9. $\dfrac{25}{45}$

Simplify to tell whether the ratios form a proportion.

10. $\dfrac{10}{60}$ and $\dfrac{2}{12}$

11. $\dfrac{10}{24}$ and $\dfrac{30}{72}$

12. $\dfrac{8}{27}$ and $\dfrac{16}{56}$

13. $\dfrac{9}{36}$ and $\dfrac{13}{40}$

14. $\dfrac{14}{27}$ and $\dfrac{42}{81}$

15. $\dfrac{15}{25}$ and $\dfrac{20}{30}$

16. $\dfrac{16}{28}$ and $\dfrac{20}{35}$

17. $\dfrac{17}{68}$ and $\dfrac{14}{56}$

18. Mr. Blackwell had two ties for every five shirts he owned. If he owned 25 shirts, how many ties did he own?

19. The school had the classroom walls painted. Seven out of 10 people surveyed liked the new color of the walls. Of the 250 people surveyed, how many people liked the new color of the walls?

Holt Middle School Math

Name _____ Date _____ Class _____

Homework and Practice
Ratios, Rates and Unit Rates

For exercises 1–3, use the bar graph to find each rate.

1. Helena's salary per week

   _____

2. Aisha's salary per day

   _____

3. Nani's salary per hour

   _____

4. Of the 405 students who took the test, 162 of them passed. Write a ratio in simplest form for the number of students who passed the test to the number of students who took the test.

   _____

**Yearly Gross Salary
Based on 52 Weeks,
5 Days a Week, 8 Hours a Day**

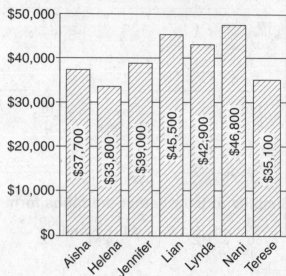

5. A lawn care company charges a homeowner $1,625 a year to maintain a lawn that is 65 ft by 50 ft. What is the maintenance fee per square foot?

   _____

6. A 12 oz container of soda has 180 calories, how many calories are in one ounce of the soda?

   _____

Determine the better buy.

7. a 500-count ream of paper for $8.25 or a 1250-count ream of paper for $20

   _____

8. a 1.5 lb bag of carrots for $2.85 or a 2 lb bag of carrots for $3.84

   _____

9. Morgan paid $16.74 for 12.4 gallons of gasoline. What was the cost per gallon?

   _____

Holt Middle School Math

Homework and Practice

LESSON 7-3

Problem Solving Skill: Analyze Units

Find the appropriate factor for each conversion.

1. millimeters to meters   **2.** inches to yards   **3.** days to minutes

_____   _____   _____

4. Oliver constructs a fence around a garden that is 24 feet by 36 feet. How many yards of fencing does Oliver need?

_____

5. Marci drinks four 48 ounce glasses of water a day. How many pints of water does she drink every day?

_____

6. Christopher wrestles for his high school in the light heavyweight division. Christopher weighs 175 pounds. How many ounces does he weigh?

_____

7. Mari bought $9\frac{1}{2}$ yards of ribbon. How many inches of ribbon did she buy?

_____

8. A bag of frozen vegetables weighs 64 ounces. How many pounds does the package of vegetables weigh?

_____

9. The 18th hole on the local golf course is 543 yards long. How many feet is the distance of this par 5 hole?

_____

A Boeing 777-300 commercial jetliner has a maximum take-off weight of 660,000 pounds, wing span of 199 feet 11 inches, overall length of 242 feet 4 inches, and an interior cabin width of 19 feet 3 inches. Find the following dimensions of the plane.

10. What is the maximum take-off weight in tons? _____

11. What is the measure of the wing span in inches? _____

12. What is the overall length of the plane in yards? _____

Holt Middle School Math

Name _____ Date _____ Class _____

Homework and Practice
Solving Proportions

Tell whether each pair of ratios are proportional.

1. $\frac{5}{6} \overset{?}{=} \frac{30}{36}$

2. $\frac{8}{20} \overset{?}{=} \frac{6}{14}$

3. $\frac{12}{27} \overset{?}{=} \frac{8}{18}$

4. $\frac{13}{15} \overset{?}{=} \frac{39}{45}$

5. $\frac{8}{16} \overset{?}{=} \frac{50}{100}$

6. $\frac{21}{49} \overset{?}{=} \frac{14}{36}$

7. $\frac{18}{24} \overset{?}{=} \frac{9}{15}$

8. $\frac{4}{18} \overset{?}{=} \frac{18}{81}$

9. $\frac{16}{10} \overset{?}{=} \frac{26}{20}$

10. $\frac{24}{14} \overset{?}{=} \frac{36}{21}$

11. $\frac{25}{16} \overset{?}{=} \frac{5}{4}$

12. $\frac{17}{11} \overset{?}{=} \frac{51}{33}$

Solve each proportion.

13. $\frac{4}{15} = \frac{a}{45}$

14. $\frac{16}{18} = \frac{8}{w}$

15. $\frac{m}{11} = \frac{32}{44}$

16. $\frac{12}{t} = \frac{4}{7}$

17. $\frac{9}{b} = \frac{27}{72}$

18. $\frac{x}{36} = \frac{21}{27}$

19. $\frac{6}{y} = \frac{18}{51}$

20. $\frac{10}{32} = \frac{15}{x}$

21. $\frac{45}{81} = \frac{n}{27}$

22. $\frac{28}{21} = \frac{44}{t}$

23. $\frac{d}{42} = \frac{49}{147}$

24. $\frac{17}{r} = \frac{102}{78}$

25. The Orlemann family planted 3 rows of corn this year and harvested 270 ears. How many rows should they plant if they want to harvest 360 ears of corn?

26. Find the number of times a heart beats in 2 minutes if it beats 576 times in 8 minutes.

27. David is making chocolate-chip cookies. Chocolate chips cost $1.79 for 12 ounces. David buys 60 ounces of chocolate chips for the cookies. How much did the chocolate chips cost?

Holt Middle School Math

Homework and Practice

Tell whether each transformation is a dilation.

1.

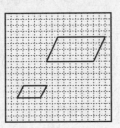

2.

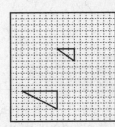

_____ _____

Dilate each figure by the given scale factor with *P* as the center of dilation.

3. scale factor is 2

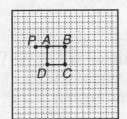

4. scale factor is $\frac{1}{3}$

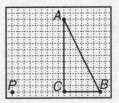

Dilate each figure by the given scale with the origin as the center of dilation. What are the coordinates of the image?

5. scale factor is 2

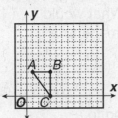

6. scale factor is $\frac{1}{3}$

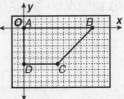

_____ _____

7. scale factor is 3

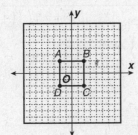

8. scale factor is $\frac{1}{4}$

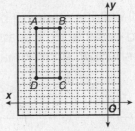

_____ _____

Holt Middle School Math

LESSON 7-6   Homework and Practice
Similar Figures

1. Which figures are similar to *ABCD*?

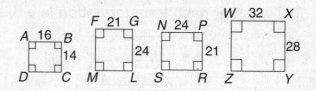

_____

_____

2. If a tree casts a 22-ft shadow at the same time a 6-ft tall person casts a 4-ft shadow, how tall is the tree?

_____

3. In $\triangle RST$, $RS = 28$ cm, $ST = 20$ cm, $RT = 24$ cm. If $\triangle DKM$ is similar to $\triangle RST$ and the ratio of the corresponding sides of $\triangle DKM$ to $\triangle RST$ is 3 to 4, find the lengths of $\overline{DK}$, $\overline{KM}$, and $\overline{DM}$.

_____

4. A nickel is approximately 20 mm in diameter and a quarter is approximately 25 mm in diameter. If the nickel is enlarged to a diameter of 128 mm, what would be the diameter of the quarter using the same scale?

_____

5. The students gave their school a gift of an American flag that measures 30 ft by 50 ft. They wanted to make a scale drawing of the flag to place on a plaque acknowledging the gift. What would the dimensions of the flag on the plaque be if it were made to a scale of 10 ft = 1 in.?

_____

6. Lilly is enlarging a photo that is 4 in. wide and 6 in. long to a photo that is 24 in. wide. What would be the length of the new photo after the enlargement?

_____

7. A 4 ft tall child is standing by The Leaning Tower of Pisa in Italy. The child casts a 15 ft shadow at the same time the tower casts a 675 ft shadow. Approximate the height of the Leaning Tower of Pisa.

_____

Holt Middle School Math

Name _____ Date _____ Class _____

Homework and Practice

Scale Drawings

The scale of a drawing is $\frac{1}{4}$ in. = 12 ft. Find the actual measurement.

1. 8 in.   **2.** 11 in.   **3.** 16 in.   **4.** 18 in.

_____   _____   _____   _____

5. 22 in.   **6.** 27 in.   **7.** 21.5 in.   **8.** 38.5 in.

_____   _____   _____   _____

The scale is 2 cm = 15 m. Find the length each measurement would be on a scale drawing.

9. 180 m   **10.** 585 m   **11.** 330 m   **12.** 420 m

_____   _____   _____   _____

13. 225 m   **14.** 622.5 m   **15.** 547.5 m   **16.** 682.5 m

_____   _____   _____   _____

17. On a map the distance between Charleston and Mt. Pleasant is 3.2 cm. The scale is 1 cm = 25 mi. What is the actual distance in miles between these two towns?

_____

18. Blueprints of a building are drawn with a scale of 1 cm = 25 ft. If the base of the building is a square with a perimeter 700 feet, what is the length of one side of the base of the building on the scale drawing?

_____

19. If the scale drawing of a room has measurements of 8 cm by 4.5 cm and the scale of the drawing is 1 cm = 8 ft, what are the actual measurements of the room?

_____

Holt Middle School Math

LESSON 7-8 Homework and Practice
Scale Models

Tell whether each scale reduces, enlarges, or preserves the size of the actual object.

1. 1 in.:15 in.   **2.** 3 ft:1 yd.   **3.** 1 cm:1 in.

_____   _____   _____

4. 40 cm:10 in.   **5.** 1,760 yd:1 mi   **6.** 1 mi:1 km

_____   _____   _____

Change both measurements to the same unit of measure, and find the scale factor.

7. 2-in. model of a 5-ft desk   **8.** 4-ft model of a 120-yd field

_____   _____

9. 30-cm model of a 7.5-m wall   **10.** 50-in. model of a 7,000-ft volcano

_____   _____

11. The museum has a 2-ft model of a 10-yard shark. What is the scale factor of the model?

_____

12. Marina made a scale model of her yard. Her yard is 40 ft × 28 ft 9 in. Her drawing is 16 in. × 11.5 in. What scale factor did she use?

_____

13. A 17 in. model of a 2002 Buick Rendezvous is made with a scale factor of $\frac{1}{11}$. Estimate the actual length of a 2002 Buick Rendezvous?

_____

14. A miniature fireplace for a dollhouse is 4.5 in. by 6.75 in. If the scale factor is $\frac{1}{12}$, what size fireplace does the miniature represent?

_____

Holt Middle School Math

Homework and Practice

Scaling 3-Dimensional Figures

A 15-in. cube is built from small cubes, each 1 in. on a side. Compare the following values.

1. the side lengths of the two cubes

   _____

   _____

2. the surface area of the two cubes

   _____

   _____

3. the volumes of the two cubes

   _____

A 20-in. cube is built from small cubes, each 1 in. on a side. Compare the following values.

4. the side lengths of the two cubes

   _____

   _____

5. the surface area of the two cubes

   _____

   _____

6. the volumes of the two cubes

   _____

7. The dimensions of a warehouse are 180 ft long, 225 ft wide, and 90 ft high. The scale model used to build the warehouse is 15 in. long. Find the width and height of the model of the warehouse.

   _____

8. A 4-cm × 3-cm × 5-cm solid figure is built with centimeter cubes. If each dimension is doubled, how many cubes are used to build the larger solid?

   _____

Holt Middle School Math

LESSON **Homework and Practice**
8-1 *Relating Decimals, Fractions, and Percents*

Find the missing ratio or percent equivalent for each letter on the number line.

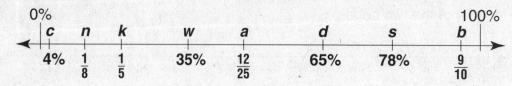

0%   100%

| c | n | k | w | a | d | s | b |

4% $\frac{1}{8}$ $\frac{1}{5}$ 35% $\frac{12}{25}$ 65%   78% $\frac{9}{10}$

1. *a*   **2.** *b*   **3.** *c*   **4.** *d*

_____   _____   _____   _____

5. *k*   **6.** *n*   **7.** *s*   **8.** *w*

_____   _____   _____   _____

Find each equivalent value.

9. 44% as a fraction   **10.** $\frac{3}{50}$ as a decimal   **11.** $\frac{13}{40}$ as a percent

_____   _____   _____

12. $\frac{3}{5}$ as a percent   **13.** $11\frac{1}{9}$% as a fraction   **14.** $\frac{3}{8}$ as a decimal

_____   _____   _____

15. At Eduardo's party, 18 friends attended but 6 friends could not come. What percent of the people invited could come to the party?

_____

16. On a math quiz, Ande answered 34 out of 40 questions correctly. What percent did she answer correctly?

_____

17. There are 300 students and 25 tables in the school cafeteria. If the students are seated equally at the tables, what percent of the students are seated at one table?

_____

Holt Middle School Math

Name _____ Date _____ Class _____

LESSON 8-2 Homework and Practice
Finding Percents

Find each percent.

1. What percent of 60 is 45?

_____

2. 45 is what percent of 90?

_____

3. What percent of 45 is 18?

_____

4. What percent of 75 is 15?

_____

5. 21 is what percent of 84?

_____

6. 51 is what percent of 85?

_____

7. What percent of 60 is 27?

_____

8. What percent of 90 is 27?

_____

9. 18 is what percent of 60?

_____

10. 24.2 is what percent of 110?

_____

11. What percent of 42 is 35?

_____

12. What percent of 64 is 24?

_____

13. What percent of 78 is 27.3?

_____

14. 105 is what percent of 60?

_____

15. An airplane completed 900 miles of a 1200-mile flight.
What percent of the trip remains to be completed?

_____

16. Cloe had 36 of the 45 questions on the math test correct.
What percent of problems did Cloe have correct?

_____

17. Lincoln received $55 for his birthday. He puts $22 of it in his
savings account. What percent of the money did Lincoln deposit
in his savings account?

_____

18. Chico bought a jacket for $42. The cost of the jacket including tax,
was $44.31. What was the percent of sales tax on the purchase?

_____

Holt Middle School Math

Name _____ Date _____ Class _____

Homework and Practice
Finding a Number When the Percent Is Known

Find each number.

1. 25% of what number is 12?

_____

2. 27 is 54% of what number?

_____

3. 51 is 60% of what number?

_____

4. 32% of what number is 8?

_____

5. 80% of what number is 16?

_____

6. 76 is 95% of what number?

_____

7. 27 is 18% of what number?

_____

8. 24% of what number is 72?

_____

9. 104 is 65% of what number?

_____

10. 12 is 3% of what number?

_____

11. 5% of what number is 12.2?

_____

12. 16% of what number is 4.8?

_____

13. 90 is $66\frac{2}{3}$% of what number?

_____

14. 40.5 is 150% of what number?

_____

15. Meredith bought a bicycle that cost $385.89. In addition, she had to pay 7% sales tax on her purchase. What was the amount of sales tax Meredith paid? Round the answer to the nearest cent.

_____

16. Wilson answered 92% of a 25 question test correctly. How many questions did he answer correctly?

_____

17. Rodriquez had $84.60 of his salary withheld for taxes. This was 15% of his gross pay. What is his gross pay?

_____

18. A car dealer receives an order of 340 new cars. Thirty percent of the cars are silver in color. How many of the cars received by the dealership are silver?

_____

Holt Middle School Math

Name _____ Date _____ Class _____

Homework and Practice
Percent Increase and Decrease

Find each percent increase or decrease to the nearest percent.

1. from 16 to 12

_____

2. from 40 to 46

_____

3. from 20 to 26

_____

4. from 50 to 38

_____

5. from 75 to 45

_____

6. from 30 to 45

_____

7. from 27 to 35.1

_____

8. from 35 to 22.75

_____

9. from 84 to 54.6

_____

10. from 35 to 42.7

_____

11. from 39 to 97.5

_____

12. from 108 to 86.4

_____

13. from 63 to 39

_____

14. from 81 to 124

_____

15. from 72 to 98

_____

16. The regular price of track shoes is $49.75. They are on sale for
$39.80. What is the percent of decrease for the sale price?

_____

17. An electronics store pays a $255.50 for a TV and sells it for
$357.70. What is the percent of increase in the price of the TV?

_____

18. The Globe Company has laid off 1,220 employees of the
company's 24,400 employees. What is the percent of decrease in
the company's work force?

_____

19. Brooke is given a 4% raise which makes her salary $754 a week.
What was Brooke's salary before the salary increase?

_____

20. Clyde weighed 200 pounds and lost 15 pounds. What was the
percent of decrease in his weight?

_____

Holt Middle School Math

Homework and Practice

LESSON 8-5

Estimating with Percents

Estimate.

1. 26 out of 51

_____

2. 24% of 42

_____

3. 19% of 20

_____

4. 30% of 73

_____

5. 68% of 103

_____

6. 61 out of 82

_____

7. 32 out of 98

_____

8. 34 out of 84

_____

9. 50% of 19.6

_____

Estimate each number or percent.

10. 10% of 81.2 is about what number?

_____

11. 18 is 26% of about what number?

_____

12. About what number is 33% of 46?

_____

13. 32 is 39% of about what number?

_____

14. On Tuesday, 453 students attend school. This is about 91% of the total enrollment. Estimate the school's total enrollment.

_____

15. Suzette bought dinner for her friends. The total cost of the meals was $73.95. Suzette left a tip of $15. Approximate the percent of the tip to the cost of the meals.

_____

16. Of the 294 students who took the state test, 31 of them must retake the test. Estimate the percent of students who need to retake the test.

_____

17. The usual markup on shoes at Fast Times Department Store is 240%. During a 25%-off sale, the store sold a pair of shoes for $39.95. Estimate the amount of the store's profit on the shoes.

_____

Holt Middle School Math

Homework and Practice

LESSON 8-6

Applications of Percents

Complete the table to find the amount of sales tax for each sale amount to the nearest cent.

1.

	6% sales tax	7% sales tax	5.5% sales tax
$53.50			
$80.50			
$219.95			
$2,640.00			

Complete the table to find the commission for each sale amount to the nearest cent.

2.

	5% commission	8% commission	7.5% commission
$365.00			
$2,140.00			
$16,300.00			
$94,750.00			

3. Mr. Darney bought a house for $58,000. He made a down payment of 20% and got a loan for the rest. What was the amount of his loan?

_____

4. Elijah buys three pens for $1.89 each and a notebook for $3.95. The sales tax rate is 6%. What is Elijah's total cost? Round the answer to the nearest cent.

_____

5. Seth is a real estate agent. He receives 8% commission on the selling price of any home he sells. If the last house he sold had a selling price of $145,900, what was Seth's commission?

_____

Holt Middle School Math

LESSON 8-7 **Homework and Practice**
Simple Interest

Find the missing value.

1. principal = $175
   rate = 4%
   time = 5 years
   interest = ?

   _____

2. principal = ?
   rate = 6%
   time = 6 years
   interest = $81

   _____

3. principal = $210
   rate = 5%
   time = ? years
   interest = $31.50

   _____

4. principal = $125
   rate = ?%
   time = 4 years
   interest = $35

   _____

5. principal = ?
   rate = $5\frac{1}{4}$%
   time = 2 years
   interest = $126

   _____

6. principal = ?
   rate = 6.5%
   time = 3 years
   interest = $165.75

   _____

7. Scott deposits $1,000 in an account that earns 5% simple interest. What will the account be worth after two years?

   _____

8. A bank pays 5.5% simple interest per year. Find the total amount at the end of one year on a principal of $3,000.

   _____

9. Mr. Womer borrowed $1,100 to start his own business. National Bank charged him 15% interest per year. Mr. Womer paid $330 in interest. For what period of time did he borrow the money?

   _____

10. Ms. Lang borrows $2,300 for 30 months at 13% interest per year. How much interest will Ms. Lang pay? What is the total amount she will repay?

   _____

Holt Middle School Math

LESSON
9-1

Homework and Practice
Probability

The following table indicates the
inventory totals for a shoe store. Find
the probability for choosing the
following types of shoes.

	Two-Tone	Black	White
High-Top	25	54	21
Low Cut	15	24	11

1. P(two-tone high-top)

2. P(black low cut)

3. P(white high top)

_____

_____

_____

4. P(black shoe)

5. P(two-tone)

6. P(two-tone low cut)

_____

_____

_____

7. P(blue shoe)

8. P(black or white)

9. P(low cut or high top)

_____

_____

_____

Find the probability of drawing the following colored candies
from a jar containing 25 red, 15 blue, 20 green, 30 yellow, and
10 orange pieces of candy.

10. P(yellow)

11. P(red)

12. P(orange)

13. P(blue)

_____

_____

_____

_____

14. P(purple)

15. P(blue or green)

16. P(candy)

17. P(red or yellow)

_____

_____

_____

_____

18. There are 25 red, 16 green, 30 purple, 14 white, 20 black, and
15 orange marbles in a bag. What is the probability of picking a
marble that is not purple?

_____

19. What is the probability of tossing a 4 on a regular numerical
cube?

_____

Holt Middle School Math

LESSON 9-2 Homework and Practice
Experimental Probability

1. A number cube was thrown 125 times. The results are shown in the table below. Complete the table with the experimental probability for each outcome.

Outcome	1	2	3	4	5	6
Frequency	15	25	20	26	18	21
Probability	12%					

The school spirit wear shop sells special sweatshirts with the school logo imprinted on them in sizes small, medium, large, x-large and xx-large. In the first hour the store is open, the first 50 customers buy 2 small, 4 medium, 5 large, 15 x-large, and the rest buy xx-large. Find the probability of the purchase of each of the different size sweatshirts from the store.

2. P(x-large sweatshirt)

_____

3. P(medium sweatshirt)

_____

4. P(xx-large sweatshirt)

_____

5. P(small or large sweatshirt)

_____

If the store has 225 customers in the second hour they are open, predict how many sweatshirts of each size will be sold based on the purchases during the first hour.

6. number of small sweatshirts sold

_____

7. number of medium sweatshirts sold

_____

8. number of xx-large sweatshirts sold

_____

9. number of large and x-large sweatshirts sold

_____

10. Jay practiced his foul shots for the upcoming basketball game. He attempted 45 shots and made 36 of them. What is the probability that Jay would make the foul shot?   _____

11. If Jay took 20 foul shots in the basketball game, predict how many shots he would make based on his practicing.   _____

Holt Middle School Math

Homework and Practice

Problem Solving Strategy: Use a Simulation

Use the table of random numbers for the problems below.

2596	3623	1053	2161	8550	9672	1044	9852	8935	8727
2393	1231	2795	2036	5138	7488	5814	2086	5397	8073
5086	9057	2050	7424	1706	1391	3585	3124	4164	9498
3274	5099	1789	7021	5636	2404	7180	3395	4734	0395
1387	7460	9196	0463	1388	5104	6408	7463	3289	9321
5891	8081	6222	9656	5606	8739	8698	3982	4974	9961
1544	2817	5296	1340	9750	3943	5697	1585	1097	8365
0442	3881	9080	7964	9357	8202	9987	5681	1288	7894
7170	4188	7099	7590	2158	0242	5299	4095	6986	3935
6039	5890	3996	0217	4045	6545	3744	8368	2034	8670

Ms. Patrick gave the same math test to all three of her math classes. In the first two classes, 70% of the students received a grade above C. Estimate the probability that at least 13 of 20 students will receive a grade above C in the third class.

1. Using the first row as the first trial, count the successful outcomes and name the unsuccessful outcomes.

   _____

2. Using the second row, count the successful outcomes and name the unsuccessful outcomes.

   _____

Determine the successful outcomes in the remaining rows of the random number table.

3. third row   4. fourth row   5. fifth row   6. sixth row

_____   _____   _____   _____

7. seventh row   8. eighth row   9. ninth row   10. tenth row

_____   _____   _____   _____

11. Based on the simulation, estimate the probability that at least 13 of 20 students will receive a grade above C.

_____

Holt Middle School Math

Homework and Practice
Theoretical Probability

An experiment consists of rolling two fair dice. Find each probability.

1. P(total shown = 4)

2. P(total shown = 6)

3. P(total shown = 10)

_____ _____ _____

4. P(total shown = 11)

5. P(total shown = 1)

6. P(total shown = 5)

_____ _____ _____

7. P(total shown ≥ 2)

8. P(total shown ≤ 7)

9. P(total shown > 8)

_____ _____ _____

Find the theoretical probability of having a thrown dart land in the indicated area.

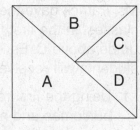

10. P(landing in area A)

11. P(landing in area B)

_____ _____

12. P(landing in area C)

13. P(landing in area D)

14. P(landing in areas A or C)

_____ _____ _____

15. What is the theoretical probability of winning a raffle if 375 tickets were sold and you bought 25?

_____

16. The second place winner of the raffle could choose between 12 envelopes each with money in them. Two of the envelopes contained a $20 bill, 4 contained $10 bills, and 6 contained $5 bills. What is the theoretical probability that the winner will choose an envelope with a $20 bill in it?

_____

Holt Middle School Math

Homework and Practice

LESSON
9-5   *The Fundamental Counting Principle*

**School identification codes at Truman School contain 1 letter
followed by 3 numbers. All codes are equally likely.**

1. Find the number of possible identification codes.

   _____

2. Find the probability that an ID code of the school does not
   contain the number 0.

   _____

3. The Dairy King Shop serves 3 flavors of ice cream: vanilla,
   chocolate, and vanilla/chocolate swirl. The ice cream can be
   served in a dish, sugar cone, or waffle cone and may be a small,
   medium, large, or jumbo size. Make a tree diagram indicating
   the possible outcomes for each ice cream served.

4. How many different ice cream selections does the Dairy King
   Shop have?

   _____

**Find the probability for each of the following. Assume all
selections are equally likely.**

5. P(dish of ice cream)   6. P(vanilla and small ice cream)

   _____   _____

7. P(medium size)   8. P(not a dish)

   _____   _____

75   Holt Middle School Math

LESSON 9-6

Homework and Practice

Permutations and Combinations

Evaluate each expression.

1. 12!

2. 9!

3. 13! − 10!

_____

_____

_____

4. 11! − 8!

5. $\frac{22!}{19!}$

6. $\frac{20!}{15!}$

_____

_____

_____

7. $\frac{18!}{(24-12)!}$

8. $\frac{21!}{(21-5)!}$

9. $\frac{17!}{(23-14)!}$

_____

_____

_____

10. How many different 3 people committees can be formed from a group of 25 people?

_____

11. From a class of 28 students, how many different ways can 4 students be selected to serve on the student council as president, vice president, secretary and treasurer?

_____

12. The boys' volleyball team has 24 players. If the coach chooses 9 boys to play at a time, how many different teams can be formed?

_____

13. The golf tournament has 120 players signed up to play. How many different 4-person sets can be formed?

_____

14. Mr. Cruz bought new tires for his car. The dealer advised Mr. Cruz to have the tires rotated every 5,000 miles. If Mr. Cruz takes the advice of the dealer and has the tires rotated a different way every 5,000 miles, how many possible miles would he drive before using all the possible rotations?

_____

Holt Middle School Math

LESSON 9-7 Homework and Practice
Independent and Dependent Events

Determine if the events are dependent or independent.

1. spinning a spinner and rolling a numerical cube

    _____

2. drawing a card from a deck and not replacing it and then drawing another card

    _____

3. selecting a piece of cake and selecting a drink

    _____

A jar contains 4 white chips, 5 purple chips, and 1 black chip. Chips are selected randomly one at a time, and are not replaced. Find the probability of the following.

4. P(purple then black)   5. P(black then white)   6. P(white then purple)

    _____   _____   _____

7. P(purple then white)   8. P(2 whites)   9. P(2 purples)

    _____   _____   _____

10. P(2 black chips)   11. P(white, then purple,   12. P(3 whites)
                                 then black)

    _____   _____   _____

13. Mrs. Benedict offers extra credit when she gives a math test. She writes the first 5 prime numbers on 5 separate cards and places them in a box. Students are permitted to draw one card to determine their extra credit when the test is finished. The cards are replaced after each student draws. What is the most extra credit a student can receive on a test? What is the probability of drawing that card?

    _____

Homework and Practice

Odds

1. If the probability of Courtney winning the raffle is $\frac{7}{12}$, what are the odds in favor of Courtney winning the raffle?

   _____

2. The odds in favor of the New York Yankees winning the World Series are 5 to 3. What is the probability that the Yankees will win the World Series?

   _____

A bag contains 18 red jelly beans, 12 green jelly beans, 10 purple jelly beans, 6 yellow jelly beans, and 4 orange jelly beans.

3. Find P(green jelly bean)   4. Find P(red jelly bean)   5. Find P(yellow jelly bean)

   _____   _____   _____

6. Find the odds in favor of choosing a red jelly bean.

   _____

7. Find the odds against choosing a red jelly bean.

   _____

8. Find the odds in favor of choosing an orange jelly bean.

   _____

9. Find the odds against choosing a purple jelly bean.

   _____

10. Find the odds in favor of choosing a green jelly bean.

    _____

11. Find the odds against choosing a yellow jelly bean.

    _____

12. Find the odds in favor of not choosing an orange jelly bean.

    _____

Holt Middle School Math

LESSON 10-1 Homework and Practice
Solving Two-Step Equations

Write and solve a two-step equation to answer the following questions.

1. Sue wants to buy a new printer that costs $189. She has $125 saved. She has a job that pays $8 an hour. How many hours must she work to earn enough to buy the printer?

_____

_____

_____

_____

_____

2. Corbin's car payment is $289. This is $37 less than $\frac{1}{3}$ of his monthly income. What is Corbin's monthly income?

_____

_____

_____

_____

_____

Solve.

3. $13 = 3a - 14$

_____

4. $\frac{1}{3}k - 4 = 1$

_____

5. $-8 = \frac{x}{3} - 5$

_____

6. $6 - 5d = 1$

_____

7. $15y + 9 = -36$

_____

8. $\frac{1}{4}x + 6 = 11$

_____

9. $\frac{w}{4} - 9 = -3$

_____

10. $0.3m - 5 = 7$

_____

11. $\frac{x - 5}{7} = -3$

_____

12. $7 - \frac{a}{4.2} = 3.5$

_____

13. $\frac{5r - 3}{2} = -4$

_____

14. $-12.9 = 5.7 + 3d$

_____

15. Nineteen more than five times a number is eighty-four. Find the number.

_____

16. Mr. Cruz buys some wood and pays $245. Each bundle of wood costs $15 and there is a delivery charge of $35. How many bundles of wood did Mr. Cruz buy?

_____

Holt Middle School Math

Homework and Practice
Solving Multistep Equations

Solve.

1. $8y - 4 - 7y = 11$ **2.** $2x + 2 + 5x = 23$ **3.** $8 = 7a - 8 - 3a$

_____   _____   _____

4. $r + 5r + 5 = -25$ **5.** $9w - 12w - 2 = 7$ **6.** $38 = 24 - 7x + 5x$

_____   _____   _____

7. $\frac{2}{7}y - \frac{5}{6} + \frac{5}{7}y = 1\frac{1}{6}$ **8.** $\frac{5}{8}x + 1 - \frac{7}{8}x = \frac{3}{4}$ **9.** $6x + 16 - 15x = -11$

_____   _____   _____

10. $\frac{4}{9}w + 6 - \frac{1}{3}w = 4$ **11.** $0.05d - 0.2d - 17 = 13$ **12.** $0.6m - 4.4 - 4.8m = 2.4$

_____   _____   _____

13. $8.2s + 4 - 13.7s = -7$ **14.** $11y - 7.5 - 6y = 2$ **15.** $13x - 4.6x - 3.9 = 8.7$

_____   _____   _____

16. The measure of an angle is 34° less than its supplement. Find the measure of each angle.

_____

17. The measure of an angle is 9° more than twice its complement. Find the measure of each angle.

_____

18. If the perimeter of the triangle is 139. Find the measure of each side.

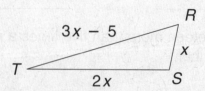

_____

Holt Middle School Math

Homework and Practice

LESSON 10-3

Solving Equations with Variables on Both Sides

Solve.

1. $5x - 1 = 21 + 3x$

2. $9y + 3 = 6y - 15$

3. $7w - 3 = w - 12.6$

_____   _____   _____

4. $12 + 8a = 3a - 3$

5. $\frac{2}{9}n - 5 = 2 + \frac{5}{9}n$

6. $1.8d + 31 = 3.4d + 19$

_____   _____   _____

7. $2b + 30 = 4b + 3$

8. $4x + 2.3 = 2x - 3.7$

9. $3(m - 5) = m - 7$

_____   _____   _____

10. $5(3h - 2) = 2(h + 8)$

11. $5 + \frac{1}{2}y = \frac{3}{8}y + 6$

12. $2\left(x - \frac{1}{2}\right) = 4\left(x + \frac{1}{4}\right)$

_____   _____   _____

13. $4(3r - 2) = 4 - 12r$

14. $\frac{1}{4}x - 7 = \frac{1}{3}x + 8$

15. $\frac{3a - 4}{2} = 5 - 2a$

_____   _____   _____

16. Mandy and Mackenzie spent the same amount of money at the arcade. They both played the same number of games. Mandy played $0.50 games and spent $10 on refreshments. Mackenzie played $0.75 games and spent $6 on refreshments. How many games did each person play?

_____

17. The square and the equilateral triangle at the right have the same perimeter. Find the lengths of the sides of the square.

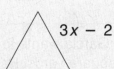

$2x + 1$

$3x - 2$

_____

Holt Middle School Math

Name _____ Date _____ Class _____

Homework and Practice
10-4 *Solving Multistep Inequalities*

Solve and graph.

1. $5x + 3 \geq 28$

_____

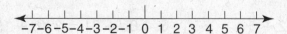

2. $10 - \frac{1}{2}w > 12$

_____

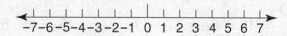

3. $7y - 15 - 4y \leq -18$

_____

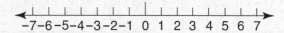

4. $7a < 12a + 10$

_____

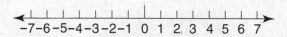
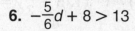

5. $19 - 4m > 4m + 11$

_____

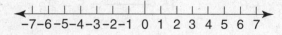

6. $-\frac{5}{6}d + 8 > 13$

_____

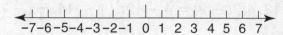
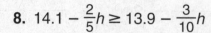

7. $2(3x + 1) \leq 4(2x - 3)$

_____

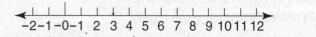

8. $14.1 - \frac{2}{5}h \geq 13.9 - \frac{3}{10}h$

_____

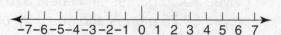

9. Six more than three-fourths a number is greater than or equal to
one more than twice the number. Find the number.

_____

10. Ms. Garcia wants to carpet her bedroom which requires
24 square yards. Her budget will allow her to spend no more
than $600 for the project. If the installation of the carpet will cost
$162, what is the most she can pay per square yard for the
carpeting?

_____

Holt Middle School Math

Name _____ Date _____ Class _____

Solve each equation for the indicated variable.

1. If the formula of changing Celsius, C, temperature to Fahrenheit, F, temperature is $C = \frac{5}{9} \times (F - 32)$, solve for F.

_____

2. If the formula for a man's shoe size, s, is $s = 3f - 24$, where f is the foot length in inches, solve for f.

_____

3. If the volume of a cylinder is $V = \pi r^2 h$, where r is the radius of the base and h is the height of the cylinder, solve for h.

_____

Solve each equation for y and graph.

4. $2x + y = 3$

_____

5. $2y - 6x = -8$

_____

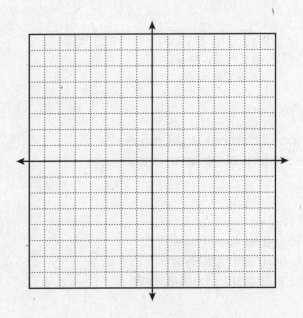

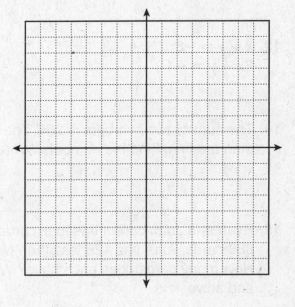

Holt Middle School Math

Homework and Practice
Systems of Equations

Determine if the ordered pair is a solution of each system of equations.

1. $(-1, 3)$
$y = -x + 2$
$y = x + 4$

_____

2. $(1, 2)$
$y = 2x$
$y - x = 1$

_____

3. $(3, 5)$
$x - y = 8$
$x + y = -2$

_____

4. $(-1, -4)$
$x = 4y$
$3x + 4y = -4$

_____

5. $(2, 4)$
$3x + 2y = 14$
$2x = y$

_____

6. $(-2, -8)$
$2x + y = 4$
$3x + y = 2$

_____

7. $(-1, 2)$
$3x + y = 1$
$6x + 2y = -2$

_____

8. $(0, 0)$
$y = 3x - 4$
$y - 3x = -4$

_____

9. $(1, -3)$
$2x = y + 5$
$2x + y = -1$

_____

Solve each system of equations.

10. $x + y = 12$
$x - y = 0$

_____

11. $2x + y = 10$
$x - y = -4$

_____

12. $x + y = -8$
$2x - y = -4$

_____

13. $3x + 2y = 0$
$x + 2y = 8$

_____

14. The sum of two numbers is 206. The second number is 48 more than the first. Find the numbers. Write a system of equations and solve.

_____

15. Ryan and Juan collect baseball cards. Together they have 880 cards. Juan has 125 less than twice as many as Ryan. How many cards does each have? Write a system of equations and solve.

_____

_____

Holt Middle School Math

Homework and Practice

LESSON 11-1 *Graphing Linear Equations*

Graph each equation and tell whether it is linear.

1. $y = -3x - 4$

x	−3x − 4	y	(x, y)
−4			
−3			
−2			
−1			
0			
1			
2			

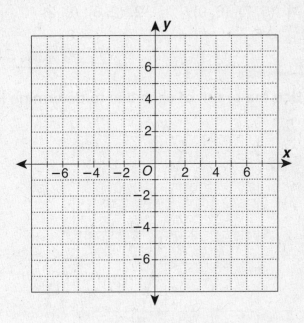

_____

2. $y = x^2 + 2$

x	x² + 2	y	(x, y)
−3			
−2			
−1			
0			
1			
2			
3			

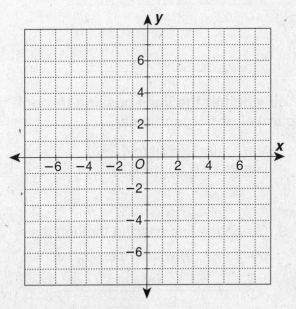

_____

3. A pharmaceutical representative sells $48,000 in a one month period. The rep earns 5.5% commission plus base salary of $400 a month. How much is the rep paid that month?

_____

Holt Middle School Math

Name _____ Date _____ Class _____

Homework and Practice
11-2 *Slope of a Line*

Find the slope of the line passing through each pair of points.

1. (5, 7), (6, 9)   **2.** (2, 8), (8, 2)   **3.** (−2, 6), (−2, −4)   **4.** (−8, −7),
                                                                                (−9, −1)

_____   _____   _____   _____

Use the graph of each line to determine its slope.

5.

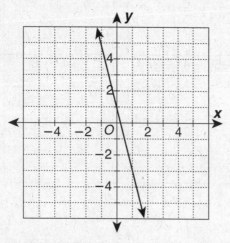

6.

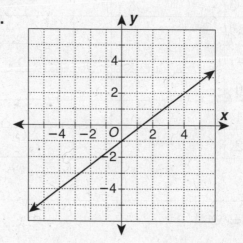

_____   _____

**Tell whether the lines passing through the given points are
parallel or perpendicular.**

7. line 1: (−1, −2), (−4, −8)
line 2: (−6, 7), (−7, 5)

8. line 1: (6, 8), (6, 10)
line 2: (−5, −9), (3, −9)

_____   _____

9. Graph the line passing through the
point (−1, 4) with slope $-\frac{1}{2}$.

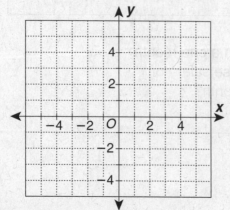

10. Graph the line passing through the
point (1, −3) with slope 3.

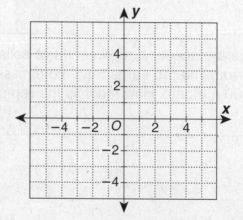

Holt Middle School Math

LESSON **Homework and Practice**
11-3 *Using Slopes and Intercepts*

Find the *x*-intercept and *y*-intercept of each line. Use the intercepts to graph the equation.

1. $x = y + 5$

2. $3x - 2y = 6$

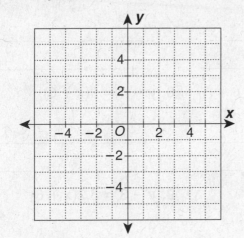

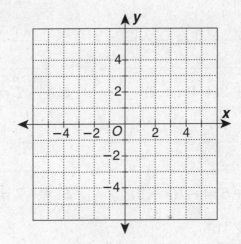

_____

_____

Write each equation in slope-intercept form and then find the slope and *y*-intercept.

3. $2x = y - 4$

4. $4x - 3y = -9$

5. $x - 4y = 8$

_____   _____   _____

Write the equation of the line that passes through each pair of points in slope-intercept form.

6. $(-1, 7), (4, -3)$

7. $(2, 5), (-8, 15)$

8. $(8, 4), (-10, -5)$

_____   _____

9. Thad's father gives him $10 for a passing report card plus $5 for every grade of A. Write an equation of a line in slope-intercept form to express *y*, the amount received with *x* grades of A. State the slope, *x*-intercept, and *y*-intercept of the equation.

_____

Holt Middle School Math

Name _____ Date _____ Class _____

Homework and Practice
11-4 *Point-Slope Form*

Identify a point the line passes through and the slope of the line, given the point-slope form of the equation.

1. $y - 6 = 3(x - 2)$

2. $y + 4 = -2(x + 1)$

3. $y - 5 = -1(x - 8)$

_____

_____

4. $y + 3 = 4(x + 2)$

5. $y - 7 = -6(x - 1)$

6. $y - 4 = 9(x + 6)$

_____

_____

7. $y + 5 = -7(x - 9)$

8. $y - 7 = \frac{1}{3}(x + 9)$

9. $y - 3 = 3.2(x + 8)$

_____

_____

Write the point-slope form of the equation with the given slope that passes through the indicated point.

10. the line with slope -3 passing through (4, 3)

11. the line with slope -1 passing through (6, -2)

_____

12. the line with slope 5 passing through (-7, 1)

13. the line with slope 7 passing through (-8, -4)

_____

14. the line with slope 2 passing through (-9, -6)

15. the line with slope -8 passing through (7, -3)

_____

16. Write an equation of a line in point-slope form that is parallel to $y = -4x + 7$ and passes through the (8, -5)

_____

Holt Middle School Math

Name _____ Date _____ Class _____

Make a graph to determine whether the data set shows direct variation.

1.

x	y
4	3
8	6
0	0
−4	−3

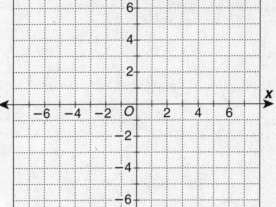

_____

_____

2. Write the equation of direct variation for exercise 1.

_____

Find each equation of direct variation, given that y varies directly with x.

3. y is 27 when x is 3

_____

4. y is 8 when x is −40

_____

5. y is −54 when x is −12

_____

6. y is 21 when x is 49

_____

7. y is −31.5 when x is 14

_____

8. y is 180 when x is −216

_____

9. Bridgett's gross pay per year is $40,300. Her net pay is $27,001 as a result of her payroll deductions. Last year Bridgett's gross salary was $37,700. Her net pay was $25,259. Write an equation of direct variation indicating Bridgett's gross pay, x, versus her net pay, y.

_____

Holt Middle School Math

LESSON **Homework and Practice**
11-6 *Graphing Inequalities in Two Variables*

Graph each inequality.

1. $y \leq 3x - 4$

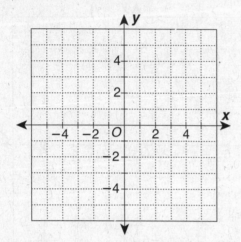

2. $y + 2x > 5$

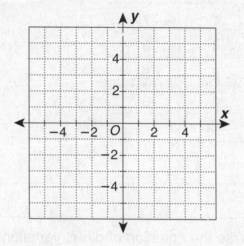

3. $x - 3y > 9$

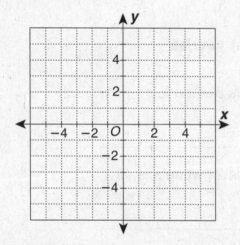

4. $-3x - y \leq 1$

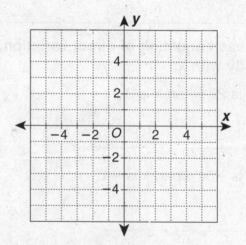

5. Richard must buy clothes for his new job. He has a budget of $250. The shirts he plans on buying cost $15 and the slacks costs $30. Let x equal the number of shirts and y equal the number of pairs of slacks Richard can buy with his clothes allowance. Write an inequality for this information.

_____

6. If Richard buys 4 pairs of slacks, what is the most number of shirts he can buy?

_____

Holt Middle School Math

Homework and Practice

Lines of Best Fit

Plot the data and find a line of best fit.

1.

x	2	4	6	8	10	12	14	16
y	12	14	18	16	20	21	25	26

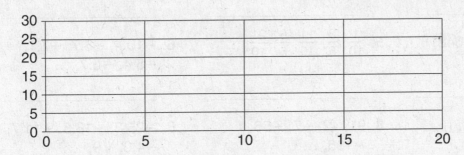

2.

x	5	10	18	20	25	30	35	40
y	135	120	105	90	94	56	50	30

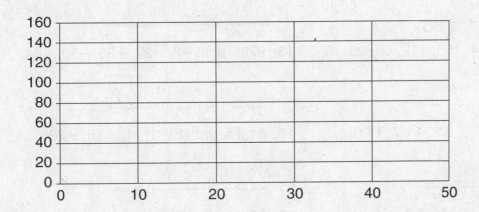

3. Nuxhall Company wants to predict their payroll costs for the next
   two years based on the salary cost over the past six years. Use
   the information in the table below and a line of best fit to
   estimate the payroll costs for the next two years.

x	Year 1	Year 2	Year 3	Year 4	Year 5	Year 6
y	$96,750	$104,490	$112,925	$125,150	$131,650	$148,825

Holt Middle School Math

Homework and Practice
Arithmetic Sequences

Determine if each sequence could be arithmetic. If so, give the common difference.

1. −19, −16, −13, −10, −7, …

2. 7, 14, 28, 56, 112, …

3. 8, 1, −6, − 13, − 20, …

_____ _____ _____

4. 1, 2.2, 4.84, 10.648, 23.4256 …

5. $\frac{1}{10}, \frac{3}{5}, \frac{11}{10}, \frac{8}{5}, \frac{21}{10}, \ldots$

6. −10.4, −8.7, −7.1, −5.4, −3.7, …

_____ _____ _____

7. $\frac{1}{8}, \frac{1}{4}, \frac{3}{8}, \frac{1}{2}, \frac{5}{8}, \ldots$

8. 91, 42, −7, −56, −105, …

9. −25.3, −18.5, −11.7, −4.9, 1.9, …

_____ _____ _____

Find the given term in each arithmetic sequence.

10. 15th term: 35, 42, 49, 56, 63, …

11. 28th term: −41, −29, −17, −5, 7, …

_____ _____

12. 32nd term: 204, 158, 112, 66, 20, …

13. 97th term: −8, −22, −36, −50, −64, …

_____ _____

14. 45th term: 3, 5.9, 8.8, 11.7, 14.6, …

15. 61st term: 49, 31, 13, −5, −23, …

_____ _____

16. 74th term: 84, 62, 40, 18, −4, …

17. 37th term: $\frac{1}{9}, \frac{4}{9}, \frac{7}{9}, 1\frac{1}{9}, 1\frac{4}{9}, \ldots$

_____ _____

18. Write the first six terms in an arithmetic sequence that begins with −8.7 and has a common difference of −3.9.

_____

20. Corrine starts a book collection by purchasing seven books. Each week she adds two new books. How many weeks before Corrine has 75 books in her collection?

_____

Holt Middle School Math

Name _____ Date _____ Class _____

Homework and Practice

Determine if each sequence could be geometric. If so give the common ratio.

1. 3, 15, 75, 375, 1,875, ...

2. −36, −30, −24, −18, −12, ...

3. 3, $\frac{3}{2}$, $\frac{3}{4}$, $\frac{3}{8}$, $\frac{3}{16}$, ...

_____ _____ _____

4. 850, 170, 34, 6.8, 1.36, ...

5. 6, 33, 171, 861, 4,311, ...

6. 14, 98, 686, 4,802, 33,614, ...

_____ _____ _____

7. 999, 333, 111, 99, 33, ...

8. 95, 38, $15\frac{1}{5}$, $6\frac{2}{25}$, $2\frac{54}{125}$, ...

9. 4, 22, 121, 665.5, 3,660.25, ...

_____ _____ _____

Find the given term in each geometric sequence. If necessary, round to the nearest hundredth.

10. 8th term; 4, 12, 36, 108, 324, ...

11. 5th term; $a_1 = 155$, $r = 0.6$

_____ _____

12. 7th term; 4, 14, 49, 171.5, 600.25, ...

13. 12th term; $a_1 = 0.05$, $r = 9$

_____ _____

14. 16th term; $\frac{1}{3125}$, $\frac{1}{625}$, $\frac{1}{125}$, $\frac{1}{25}$, $\frac{1}{5}$, ...

15. 9th term; $\frac{7}{9}$, $2\frac{1}{3}$, 7, 21, 63, ...

_____ _____

16. Nicholas has a picture that is 3 in. × 5 in. If he enlarges the photo by 25% five times, what are the dimensions of the new photo? Round to the nearest tenth of an inch?

_____

Holt Middle School Math

Name _____ Date _____ Class _____

Homework and Practice
12-3 *Other Sequences*

Use first and second differences to find the next three terms in each sequence.

1. 12, 13, 16, 21, 28, …

2. 4, 6, 10, 16, 24, …

_____

_____

3. $\frac{3}{4}$, $2\frac{3}{4}$, $5\frac{1}{4}$, $8\frac{1}{4}$, $11\frac{3}{4}$, …

4. 3.6, 4.1, 6.1, 9.6, 14.6, …

_____

_____

Give the next three terms in each sequence using the simplest rule you can find.

5. 1, 2, 4, 7, 11, …

6. 6, 7, 10, 15, 22, …

_____

_____

7. 2, 5, 10, 17, 26, …

8. 32, 50, 72, 98, 128, …

_____

_____

9. 400, 361, 324, 289, 256, …

10. 2.5, 10, 22.5, 40, 62.5, …

_____

_____

Find the first five terms of each sequence defined by the given rule.

11. $a_n = \frac{n^2}{2n}$

12. $a_n = \frac{n^2 + 5}{2n}$

13. $a_n = \frac{6n - 2}{n^2 + 1}$

_____   _____   _____

14. Suppose *a, b,* and *c* are three consecutive numbers in the Fibonacci sequence. Complete the following table and guess the pattern.

_____

a, b, c	ac	b²
1, 1, 2		
2, 3, 5		
5, 8, 13		
13, 21, 34		
34, 55, 89		

Holt Middle School Math

Name _____ Date _____ Class _____

Homework and Practice
Functions

Complete the table and graph each function.

1. $y = 3x + 4$

x	3x + 4	y
−3		
−2		
−1		
0		
1		

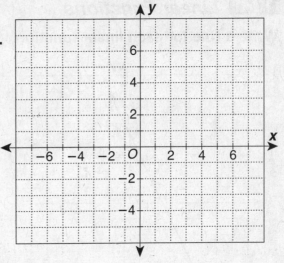

2. $y = 2x^2 - 1$

x	2x² − 1	y
−2		
−1		
0		
1		
2		

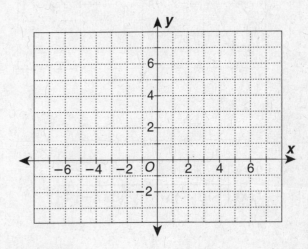

Determine if each relationship represents a function.

3. $y^2 = 4x - 3$

4.

x	2	4	6	8
y	−1	−2	−3	−4

_____   _____

5. For each function, find $f(0)$, $f(-1)$, and $f(2)$.

Function	f(0)	f(−1)	f(2)
$y = -5x + 2$			
$y = 3x^2 - 8$			

6. Given the function $f(x) = -4x^2 - 5$ and the domain
   {−3, −2, −1, 0, 1, 2, 3}. Find the range of the function.

95   **Holt Middle School Math**

LESSON
12-5

Homework and Practice
Linear Functions

Write a rule for each linear function.

1.

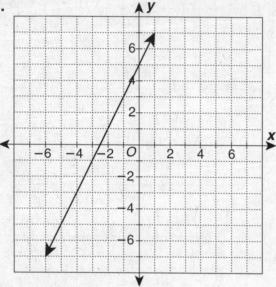

_____

2.

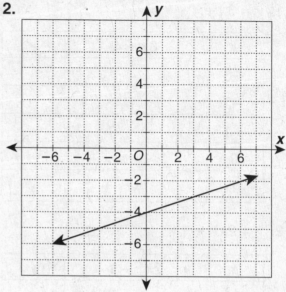

_____

3.

x	−4	−2	3	5
f(x)	13	7	−8	−14

_____

4.

x	−6	−4	2	8
f(x)	−10	−9	−6	−3

_____

5. A salesperson is paid a base salary of $300 plus 8% of their sales. Write a function rule for the salary. Graph the function.

_____

6. If a salesperson has $900 in sales, what is the salesperson's salary?

_____

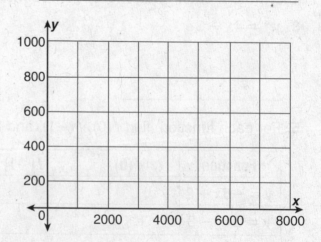

Holt Middle School Math

Name _____ Date _____ Class _____

Homework and Practice

Create a table for each exponential function, and use it to graph the function.

1. $f(x) = 0.25 \cdot 5^x$

x	y
−1	$y = 0.25 \cdot 5^{-1} = 0.05$
0	
1	
2	

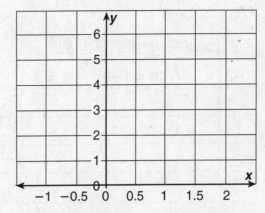

2. $f(x) = \frac{1}{4} \cdot 6^x$

x	y
−1	
0	
1	
2	

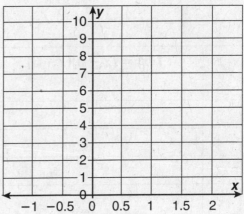

3. A lawyer opens a new office with 28 clients. She intends to increase her clientele 30% each year for the next 4 years. How many clients can she expect to have at the end of 4 years? Round the answer to the nearest whole number?

_____

4. A company owns office cars worth a total of $587,000. The cars are depreciated by 12% a year for 10 years. What is the expected value of the cars at the end of 10 years? Round the answer to the nearest cent.

_____

5. Clayton earns $725 a week at his job. He is given a 6% annual increase in pay. How much will Clayton earn per week after 3 years? Round the answer to the nearest cent.

_____

Holt Middle School Math

LESSON 12-7 Homework and Practice
Quadratic Functions

Create a table for each quadratic function and use it to make a graph.

1. $f(x) = x^2 - 6$

x	$f(x) = x^2 - 6$
−3	$f(-3) = (-3)^2 - 6 = 3$
−1	
0	
2	
3	

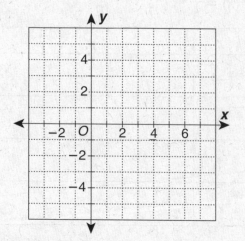

2. $f(x) = (x - 5)(x - 3)$

x	$f(x) = (x - 5)(x - 3)$
6	
5	
4	
3	
2	

3. $f(x) = x^2 - 3x - 2$

x	$f(x) = x^2 - 3x - 2$
3	
2	
1	
0	
−1	

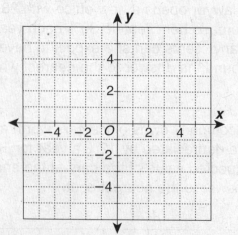

4. If the perimeter of a rectangle is 124 cm, find the dimensions of the rectangle with the greatest possible area? What is the greatest possible area?

Holt Middle School Math

Homework and Practice

LESSON 12-8 *Inverse Variation*

Tell whether each relationship is an inverse variation.

1. The table shows the length and width of a parallelogram.

Length	4	8	10	12	36
Width	18	9	7.2	6	2

2. The table shows the number of shelves and the number of books on each shelf in a library.

Number of Shelves	3	4	6	12	16
Number of Books	32	24	16	8	6

3. The table shows the number of guests at a party and the cost per guest.

Number of Guests	66	75	96	100	150
Cost per Guest	9	8	6.25	6	4

Graph each inverse variation.

4. $f(x) = \dfrac{6}{x}$

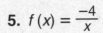

5. $f(x) = \dfrac{-4}{x}$

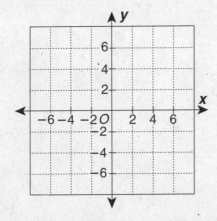

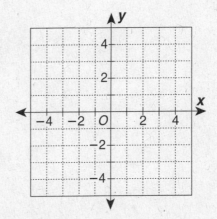

6. Hertz, abbreviated Hz, is a unit of frequency equal to 1 cycle per second. The pitch of a musical instrument is measured in vibrations per second or Hertz. If the pitch of a panpipe 2 feet long is 282 Hz, what is the length of pipe with a pitch of 376 Hz?

Holt Middle School Math

HOLT MIDDLE SCHOOL Math
Course 3

CHAPTER RESOURCE BOOKS

Student Resources
- Practice (Levels A, B, C)
- Reteach
- Challenge
- Problem Solving
- Puzzles, Twisters & Teasers
- Recording Sheets
- Chapter Review

Teacher and Parent Resources
- Chapter Planning and Pacing Guide
- Section Planning Guides
- Parent Letter
- Teaching Tools
- Teacher Support for Chapter Project
- Transparencies
    Daily Transparencies
    Additional Examples Transparencies
    Teaching Transparencies

REACHING ALL LEARNERS

English Language Learners
- Success for English Language Learners
- Math: Reading and Writing in the Content Area
- Spanish Homework and Practice
- Spanish Interactive Study Guide
- Spanish Family Involvement Activities
- Multilingual Glossary

Hands-On
- Hands-On Lab Activities
- Technology Lab Activities
- Alternate Openers: Explorations
- Family Involvement Activities

Individual Needs
- Are You Ready? Intervention and Enrichment
- Alternate Openers: Explorations
- Family Involvement Activities
- Interactive Problem Solving
- Interactive Study Guide
- Readiness Activities
- Math: Reading and Writing in the Content Area
- Challenge in CRB

Applications and Connections
- Consumer and Career Math
- Interdisciplinary Posters
- Interdisciplinary Poster Worksheets

TRANSPARENCIES

- Alternate Openers: Explorations
- Exercise Answers Transparencies

- Chapter Resource Book
    Daily Transparencies
    Additional Examples Transparencies
    Teaching Transparencies

TECHNOLOGY

Teacher Resources
- Lesson Presentations CD-ROM
- Test and Practice Generator CD-ROM
- One-Stop Planner CD-ROM

Student Resources
- Are You Ready? Intervention CD-ROM

Internet connect
- Homework Help Online
- Math Tools Online
- Glossary Online
- Chapter Project Online
- CNN Student News

KEYWORD
MT4 HWHelp
MT4 Tools
MT4 Glossary
MT4 PSProject
MT4 CNN

HOLT, RINEHART AND WINSTON
A Harcourt Education Company

ISBN 0-03-065186-7

90000

9 780030 651861